TRACKS OF DEATH
The Burma–Siam Railway

TRACKS OF DEATH

The Burma–Siam Railway

G. F. Kershaw

The Book Guild Ltd

Sussex, England

The Book Guild Ltd.
25 High Street,
Lewes, Sussex.

First published 1992
© G. F. Kershaw 1992
Set in Baskerville

Typesetting by Kudos Graphics
Slinfold, Horsham, West Sussex
Printed in Great Britain by
Antony Rowe Ltd.,
Chippenham, Wiltshire.

A catalogue record for this book is
available from the British Library

ISBN 0 86332 736 2

This book is dedicated to my beloved Jean, in pursuit of whom I defeated captivity;

and to

John Collinson of Sydney, NSW

and the late

Jan van Zanten of the Netherlands, both of whom fed me, nursed me and buttressed the will to live.

My gratitude is due to the Rev. E.I. Robertson, ex-Chindit, who knew the area, the jargon and the Japs, and who voluntarily typed the manuscript on two occasions.

CONTENTS

'Heaven from all creatures hides the book of fate,
All but the page prescribed, their present state,
From brutes what men, from men what spirits know,
Or who could suffer being here below.'

Alexander Pope

INTRODUCTION

Writing one's recollection of the war so many years after the conclusion of events may seem a hazardous enterprise: fallible memory and faulty recollection may both play a part, as may prejudice. When I commenced the diaries, on which this record is based, in 1941, it was with the idea of writing a book. The original effort had to be destroyed when the Far East war started, and it was only when I was convalescing in 1942 from dysentery and beriberi that the diary was re-commenced, more to frustrate boredom than with the idea of creating a literary masterpiece.

The intervening years have been devoted to raising a family, undertaking a demanding job and many extra-mural interests, and to several years of happy retirement; and if any excuse were needed for such a long delay it is found in the fact that the many and still-recurring nightmares provoked by any recollection of POW days – books, TV, radio and discussion included – may now be sufficiently quiescent to allow me to bring the project to a successful conclusion.

In order to avoid dwelling at too great a length on the more morbid parts of the narrative, I have shuffled the various experiences around at considerable length, and only chronology has dictated a regular pattern.

1

TROOPERS AND TRANSPORTS

When 'M' Divisional Signals left Thorpe Lea House, Egham, Surrey, on 1 January 1941, the prospect for the United Kingdom was bleak. Although the Battle of Britain had officially concluded on the 31 October 1940, and the immediate threat of invasion had passed, the Battle of the Atlantic still raged, heavy bombing occurred with great regularity on our major cities, Western Europe was under Nazi domination from the North Cape to the Spanish border, and our defence position in the Middle East was tenuous, to say the least.

My inclusion on the advance baggage party allowed me to visit a smoke-filled St Paul's Cathedral, and to see the still-burning Ludgate Hill, Pasternoster Row, and the surrounding area, all now in ruins; hardly an encouraging farewell for an overseas visit of indefinite and hazardous duration.

We stayed overnight in the war-requisitioned Grand Central Hotel, Marylebone, and on 2 January entrained at King's Cross for an unknown destination; and only those who have travelled in a wartime, blacked-out, slow-moving and overcrowded train will understand our experience.

If dimness of lighting indicates a religious enterprise we were already in the company of the cherubim and seraphim. One tiny blue light in the centre of the ceiling was sufficient to allow identification of one's immediate neighbours, and reading was totally out of the question. We were six to the compartment, dressed in battle-dress, greatcoat and boots, and carrying a valise and side-pack – these items of equipment being placed in the overhead racks. In those days most people smoked, and in a very short time the

11

compartment was in a complete fug – a condition rarely seen nowadays. When we pulled out of King's Cross at about 1400 hours on 2 January it was a grey and overcast day, and so it remained throughout the entire journey.

As with all troop trains we surrendered all priority to normal passenger traffic, and our journey north was punctuated by almost motionless crawls and frequent stops. We continued throughout the day and the following night in this hesitant progress, and at about 0700 hours on 3 January, still without any idea of our whereabouts, we were ordered to de-train. We had had little food – only sandwiches issued before we left Egham – or sleep – but jumping down to the track, handing out our kit and getting the blood circulating again brought us back to life. The weather was bitterly cold, with frost everywhere, and the fog now so dense that even the natives were unable to identify their own surroundings. We were 'fell in' and marched off across several further sets of lines, and after some moments were halted and stood at ease.

We continued to gawp above and around us at the impenetrable fog until someone said, 'There's a mast up there'. He was given the traditional services' advice with regard to seeking medical help, seeing a psychiatrist, and taking more water with it, when it was suddenly realised by many more people that he was perfectly correct. We were, in fact, standing alongside a 26,000 ton liner, the *Empress of Japan*, in Glasgow docks. It took from 0730 till 1030 hours to get us all on board, a total of 3,000 souls, as they used to say in Victorian novels; but it was our bodies we were mainly concerned with at that time: we were allocated hammocks, table tops, space under the tables, in alley-ways, and even on landings. In view of the many ships that had been sunk to date, frequently with the loss of all on board, the introduction to life-jackets and how to use them did little to encourage us. The riggings, rails and decks were all frozen solid and, even by Glaswegian meteorological standards, it was too cold to remain on deck even when we were fully dressed,and we tended to congregate increasingly in the foetid atmosphere below decks.

The inevitable result was that in a few days sixty per cent of those on board were sick. A route-march in dense fog did little to relieve the problem as the trams and other traffic proved a greater menace in the dense fog than our respiratory problems; and taking into account the possibility that it was a golden opportunity to jump ship, no further essays ashore were attempted, and we continued to sweat it out on board.

On Saturday 11 January 1941, at 1030 hours, we moved from Glasgow to Greenock where we anchored overnight after a glorious sunset, and the following day saw us sailing down the Clyde, a convoy of thirty-six merchant and Royal Navy ships, the largest at that time to have left the United Kingdom. Although all portholes remained closed, by order, the movement of the ships, added to the overworked ventilators, did much to clear the atmosphere, the food was good and we settled down to yet another tour with an unknown destination. We had of course been issued with full tropical kit before leaving Surrey, but considering the worldwide dimensions of the war and the size of the British Empire this was no more than an indication of a hot climate.

In order to avoid the packs of U-boats that kept wreaking such havoc among our shipping in the Atlantic, we sailed north-west towards the Arctic Circle, then west towards America, then south and finally the long south-east trip to Freetown in Sierra Leone, where we arrived on 24 January. With the increasing temperatures of recent days I decided on the 22nd to take my hammock and blanket-roll on deck each night and there several of us stayed until we reached our final destination. Our arrival at Freetown was observed by a Nazi reconnaisance plane, at which everything in the area with a gun fired. He flew on unperturbed, our only casualties being two servicemen hit by shell splinters, but it was an ill omen for our security when we should leave harbour.

Throughout our long zigzag trip we had been considerably encouraged by the presence of an escorting battleship and two destroyers. The latter fussed around us at all times, and we assumed they provided the necessary protective screen between us and any threatening U-boats. When we left Freetown on 25 January and headed west into the South Atlantic the three warships took up their usual stations and shortly after we turned south again the two destroyers went haring off north-west. Shortly afterwards we heard gunfire and when they returned we learnt that they had located a U-boat – and sunk it.

The further south we went the more the tension of the war eased. Although we were still blacked out overall at night the warmer weather tempted us on deck throughout the day and we were able to bathe in the deck pool and to sunbathe. Much of our time was spent in interpreting the Morse code in the ship-to-ship traffic by Aldis lamp. As most of us in my section were radio operators we always had an eager audience, particularly of officers who 'just happened' to be within earshot but who were without knowledge of the code. For their benefit we delighted in composing the most ridiculous reports, mainly concerning the war, and we often wondered what discussions took place subsequently in their mess.

On 8 February I was on duty as a mess orderly when I was asked by a friend if I had looked through a porthole recently. When I told him that I was sick of the sight of water he suggested that I think again; and there, for the first time, I saw one of the world's most magnificent natural masterpieces: Table Mountain, with its majestic sweep of bay, Kloof Buttress and the Sea Point area. After seventeen months of blacked-out England and blacked-out ship and the boredom of the voyage we felt transported to another world. We stayed there for four days, and we were overwhelmed by the hospitality of the inhabitants, the beauty and cleanliness of the city, the total absence of any evidence of war; and shocked and saddened by the squalor of the Bantu population in their shacks between Capetown and Groote Schuur, a problem unresolved all these years later! So deeply were we impressed by all that we saw that many men emigrated to that country after the war, and there they remain to the present day and are among my hosts on my visits to that wonderful land.

Our route now lay via Mombasa, where we lay in harbour overnight, Bombay where we took our first lessons on the mysterious Orient during twenty-four hours ashore, and then, accompanied only by the *Aquitania*, the dash down the Indian Ocean to Singapore.

We had known for some time that Malaya was to be our destination, and had had the usual lectures on rubber production, non-fraternising with the natives, brothels, VD, climate, food and local customs. Much of it appeared to belong to a previous century, and we suspected that some of the more eager young officers had been given the subjects to swot up so that they could appear in a more authoritative role to the men.

We disembarked at the naval base, took train to Tanglin, and then marched to the tented accommodation in the rubber plantation at Ulu Pandan. The total absence of any comfort in such conditions was probably excellent preparation for what lay ahead of us for the next four-and-a-half-years but was singularly unappreciated after two months on an overcrowded trooper. The oil lamps attracted every winged creature known in those particular tropics, tarantulas played in the ridge-poles and scorpions at our feet, and the daytime temperatures made the tents uninhabitable. To add to our pleasure we were informed that owing to possible smallpox in the area we were quarantined until further notice!

The British Army, at least, is famous for its capacity to provide occupations for its otherwise indolent troops but our tenancy of a clearing in the rubber trees presented the CO with something of a problem. No coal to whitewash, no sandbags to fill, no electrical circuits to allow the operators to practise Morse.

Our only official duty was the manning of the switchboard to allow communication with Command at Fort Canning; but as we knew noone by name, rank or unit, or their location, and as our centre of operations was a tiny tent filled with mosquitoes after dark at about 1800 hours, and as the switchboard and I were forced to push our heads through the ridge of the tent, it was a job that we hated and avoided wherever possible.

Our greatest source of pleasure at that time lay in the route marches that were arranged all too infrequently. After our long confinement to ship and tent, we longed for the exercise and the change of scene that these involved. No distance or high temperature was too great, and we were introduced to scenery and a polyglot community of British,

15

Malayans, Indians and Chinese such as those who came from the non-seafaring parts of the UK had never imagined. It was during one of these marches that a chance remark by me that the scenery reminded me of Epping Forest brought a response from a fellow forest-lover, Frank Pidgeon, that initiated a friendship that has continued to enrich my life, in many varied ways, to date.

After two weeks of unpleasant duty, boredom, exhausting heat in the tents, mosquitoes, tarantulas, scorpions, and the quagmires caused by the frequent flash storms, we were overjoyed to be given the opportunity to visit the city whose defence was our principal reason for being there – Singapore, the City of the Lion. In 120 years, since its occupation by Sir Stamford Raffles, it had been transformed from a bandit-ridden mangrove swamp to the great entrepot centre of the Far East – complete with naval base, docks, godowns, barracks, communications, and that vast cosmopolitan population that follows trade the world over, when permitted to do so. Even now I can invoke those sights, sounds and smells with ease; the rows of hanging fish and other meats with their attendant myriads of flies in windowless shops, the xylophone effect of a thousand wooden *choplis* as they struck the pavements as their owners walked, the scent of herbs and spices and joss-sticks, and cooked pork and chicken, and over all the excited chatter and childlike laughter of the local populace, the hooting of impatient horns, the squealing of protesting brakes. I wonder if modern Singapore with its hygiene and skyscrapers and robust administration is still as intriguing! Do the rickshaw pullers still ply their pressing trade to hotels, cinemas and brothels; do the opium addicts still lie in open rooms, unconscious to their intolerable poverty; do Sikh taxi-drivers still conduct vendettas as they seek clients? I doubt it.

In the intervening years, under the inspired leadership of Lee Kwan Yew, Singapore is reported to have been transformed from a city of massive wealth in the midst of an even more massive poverty, to one of scrupulously tidy hygiene – no cigarette butts or packets in the streets, no spitting, no refuse in the monsoon drains. How much that must have improved both the sights and the smells of that teeming city.

But how does the Asiatic fraternity (and sorority!) live without the traditional hawking and spitting? Quite apart from the respiratory distress caused by biddies, cheap cigarettes and tuberculosis one recalls the betelnut beloved by many Asiatics. Its position between cheek and teeth promoted dental caries, black gums and massive salivation – the evidence for the last being found in huge gobbets of saliva that stained every pavement and road.

Many of the Chinese women of those days were victims of foot-binding in infancy and girlhood, ostensibly because the result was considered beautiful. The distortion of their metatarsals was so great that they hobbled along with mincing steps. One wondered how they had coped with the carrying of children, both during and after pregnancy, and with the normal household chores involving weight-bearing with two hands. Perhaps the evidence of such a practice is no longer apparent.

By the end of March I felt it was time to find a more interesting life-style, and an opportunity presented itself in the form of a request from Command that anyone with experience of senior administration should apply for a transfer to unit HQ, Alexandra Barracks, Singapore. I applied and was interviewed and appointed; and on 29 March 1941 I was transported, bag and baggage, to that location, along with three or four others from my unit.

HQ consisted at that time of Colonel F.T. Pope, Captain R. Peel, Regimental Sergeant-Major Parker, Sergeant Ray, Corporal Wood, Corporal Thompson, Lance-Corporal Barnes, Signalmen Sandy, Pidgeon and myself. In addition there were two civilian-attached Chinese – Lee Choon Eng and Chia Soo Hiang. Pope, Ray and Wood died up-country on the Railway of Death, Peel was drowned at sea when the Japanese bombed the evacuating destroyers two days before Singapore collapsed but Parker, Barnes, Sandy and Pidgeon all survived captivity.

Despite several attempts we have been unable to trace our Chinese friends. As there was a major massacre of the Chinese population after Singapore fell it may be that they were among the victims.

If we needed a mental stimulus after our months of

17

inactivity we certainly found it now. It was apparent that the previous occupants of unit HQ had allowed it to fall into disuse, and we were detailed to re-organise it completely. Most of us had been in the army for several months only, and we relied much more on native wit than on King's Regulations or esoteric instruction for the systems we installed. As with all such offices, we covered troop movements throughout the island and to the peninsula, discipline, messing, secrets work, traffic accidents, vehicle maintenance etc. – duties that often demanded our working from 0800 to midnight. At least this allowed us to miss daily parades and physical instruction but robbed us of much of our social freedom – inter-regimental sports, visits to friends and to Singapore, and outings to cinemas and swimming pools. Nevertheless we formed a happy team in congenial surroundings: the first floor provided both office and living accommodation away from the hurly-burly of barracks, the surrounding gardens were festooned with frangipani, and two sides of the verandah overlooked trees and lawns and far open country. 'Char' was brought to us at 0730 and 1600 by the number-one boy, dear old George Ram Krishan, who lowered our mosquito nets, cleaned our shoes and brasses and did our casual shopping. He was a survivor of the Quetta earthquake, totally honest, and identified by the spoor of curry that trailed him at all times.

Singapore had been a garrison for all three services for so long that its amenities were fairly well developed. The Union Jack Club and the YMCA saw to our needs in the way of drinks, food, writing materials and homely atmosphere where we could relax in comfort. St Andrew's Cathedral and its wonderful bishop, Leonard Wilson, – soon to be almost tortured to death by the Japanese – saw both to our spiritual and material needs by way of church services succeeded by tea and biscuits, while the many Chinese and Indian cafés provided excellent food at low cost. As a guest member of Tanjong Rhu Swimming Club I was a frequent visitor there on Sundays with a friend. Our trips into the water were interspersed with drinks, tiffin and afternoon tea – all paid for by a generous sponsor, Mrs Van Zuyderhoudt, who continued our friend to the end. I wonder what happened to her!

18

But such friendships between service personnel and civilians were few and far between, and very actively discouraged by the latter. Regular troops the world over are never popular – boredom, homesickness, alcohol and women are never an attractive social foundation – but the civilians of Singapore failed to appreciate that we were conscripts, there to defend them, and had in our ranks accountants, solicitors, schoolteachers, chemists, hospital administrators, etc. No matter, the mark of the beast was on our forehead, and the ladies, at least, drew metaphorical Victorian crinolines to one side, and warned their daughters of a fate worse than death! Many of these civilians were totally unqualified and had taken off into the Empire during the years of the depression when jobs were unobtainable in England. They relied heavily on their 'colonial' status for their self-esteem and social position but many of them were parvenus whose shortcomings were revealed in their treatment of the native population and their own behaviour in public.

Alexandra and the adjacent Gillman Barracks were splendid structures built on the old colonial pattern of three storeys with wide doors to verandahs on both sides, flat roofs with large extensions at ends and sides as protection against frequent torrential rain, and beautifully-maintained gardens throughout. The roads were wide and well-lit as befitted service traffic, and there were parade and sports grounds. This pattern was repeated throughout the Island, augmented by wood-hutted accommodation which had been hastily erected when war appeared imminent in the Far East.

So far as our own barracks were concerned, Alexandra provided the lap of luxury, not only in contrast to our life in war-torn England but by general standards. All meals were prepared, cooked and cleared away by the local population (mostly Chinese), the accommodation was well decorated and lit, dhobi wallahs washed and ironed our clothes to military standards, beds consisted of the traditional telescoping two-piece sections with three 'biscuits' as a mattress, and there was an overhead mosquito net to each bed. Inter-regimental football and hockey matches were frequently arranged on our own pitches and there was boxing at Tanglin Barracks.

Mention of beds and mosquito nets reminds me of one of the less-welcome incidents that occurred at that time. During my morning shower on that first week in Alex, I noticed several circular pink marks on my left calf. When I showed these to the Orderly Room Sergeant he remarked, quite casually, 'Bugs'. Bearing in mind the response that such a diagnosis would bring in England I felt both insulted and horrified. However, we went to my iron bedstead on the verandah five yards away and when he ran his pencil between the two metal plates of the bed-head a colony of them fell on the floor. Thus I followed long-established army practice, drew a blow lamp and fuel from the QM stores, and thoroughly sterilised the entire metal-work – for a few days at least.

On a subsequent occasion I found the inside of the crown of the net laden with the wretched things. I submerged the whole net under water and disinfectant for twenty-four hours and then hung it over the cement balustrade to dry. When I eventually re-hung it the bugs ran out as chirpy and alert as though I had submerged them in the elixir of life!

The food was varied, well-cooked and plentiful, and usually accompanied by limitless lime-juice, made daily from fresh fruit, sugared and iced. Our only complaint was that meat was served at each meal, and we longed for an English tea with bread and butter, scones, tea-cake, fruit loaf, etc. I happened to mention this to one of my English hostesses and on the occasion of my next afternoon visit I was served these very items, complete with Devonshire cream and China tea – on a first-floor verandah with a wide view of the island. I have never forgotten it. The great advantage was that our messing was still on a peacetime basis and remained so almost until our collapse. This meant that each unit messing officer received a cash allowance for every man on his ration strength, to be spent without restriction. This had the added attraction that, as we were Corps Signals with more sedentary occupations than infantry, gunners, and so on, and thus apparently ate less bread, the saving on that commodity could be spent on items such as pineapples and oranges which made a further contribution to variety – and added to the opinion of visiting troops that Fortress Signals had the best mess of any, either on the island or on the peninsula!

But such excellent food, freedom of entertainment and movement (usually by taxi), and the absence of war in any of its phases made us increasingly aware of our families and friends in Britain. Having experienced the fury of the Battle of Britain and the bombing of so many areas in the UK we were acutely aware of their worsening situation. No word of complaint ever reached us from our homes, but the losses in the Middle East, the increasing violence of the Battle of the Atlantic, reports in the local press of stringent rationing, and the continuing air attacks on Britain, made us very conscious that we could do nothing in mitigation – the few parcels that we sent home never arrived and we had to assume that they had been torpedoed on the way.

As 1941 advanced there were ominous signs of an approaching conflict in the Far East. Bearing in mind that our only ally, France, had collapsed in June 1940, that Germany occupied Western Europe from the North Cape to the Spanish border, that Germany and Italy were allied against Britain, and that Britain was fighting alone, and totally committed by land, sea and air both to the defence of our islands and the war in the Middle East, it was imperative that we should avoid further involvement in any theatre. Although further contingents of troops continued to arrive we were very aware of the total inadequacy of the air force, both on the island, and on the peninsula. Those of us who had lived through the Battle of Britain recognized the tremendous qualities of Spitfires and Hawker Hunters. In Singapore there were no such values; we appeared to have only a very limited number of Brewster Buffaloes, whose single machine-gun fired through the propeller boss and whose rate of climb barely defeated gravity. Breakdowns were reported to be frequent and spares almost unobtainable, as with all superannuated equipment. The few bombers based on the island were in the same category, totally inadequate for modern operations and just as unlikely to be replaced, bearing in mind our needs in other theatres of war; and it required only a very cursory visit to the naval base and the harbour to prove that our naval units consisted mainly of small and ancient craft, some of them being only river craft transferred from the China Station. The prospects for the war that now appeared to be inevitable were bleak indeed.

On 6 October 1941 I achieved the dizzy heights of senior command by being appointed a lance-corporal, that man-of-all-work who carries the can, receives all the bricks and few of the happence and whose best efforts are plagiarised by those higher up the ladder for their greater glory.

I now took over responsibility at NCO level for messing for Alexandra Barracks, and this included units of the Ordnance and Service Corps as well as Royal Signals. This was mainly a matter of continuing the routine of my predecessor, but an amusing incident occurred that I feel is worth recording. We were still on 'peace-time messing' which meant that we were allocated cash for each man on the ration strength, as against 'war-time messing' which meant that we received only issue rations. The cash allocation was usually spent at the local NAAFI on food and drink extras.

A friend at Command 'tipped me the wink' that all messing cash-in-hand was to be recalled and that wartime messing was to be commenced. In order to frustrate this I pre-dated a cheque for the whole amount I held, swore the NAAFI manager to secrecy and placed an order with him for Christmas puddings, mince-pies, Christmas cake, beer and orange juice. When the anticipated order was published I was able to say quite truthfully that the money was spent. I was ordered to retrieve it from the NAAFI, and went through the motions, but I was determined not to give in. After two or three weeks of cat-and-mouse communication I was phoned by a colonel who stated that I was to be court-martialled for refusing to obey an order; but the Japanese had other ideas and no court was convened. I am delighted to record that the subsequent Christmas fare fulfilled everyone's expectation, a personal reward made all the greater by the knowledge that it was the last Christmas dinner that many hundreds of those men had.

2

WAR

On Saturday 7 December, 1941 I was on Signals Office duty
when I received the codeword from Command that war was
imminent. I informed everyone by phone or signal, and
then shot off to Singapore to keep the usual dinner
appointment with Tom Ireland at the London Café,
realising that this was probably to be the last occasion –
which it was. Conscience dictated that we should return to
our units as soon as possible but the remainder of the day
passed uneventfully, as the other office staff had now
moved to Fort Canning (Command HQ); and RSM Parker,
Bill Thompson and I got into out beds, and prepared for a
good night's sleep.

At 0400 hours on the following day we were awakened by
fairly heavy aerial activity which was followed shortly· by
several loud explosions. The RSM assured me that this was
RAF practice bombing but in answer to my question he
assured me that, after nineteen years in the army, he had
never heard a bomb dropped in anger. I assured him that
thanks to the Battle of Britain and the frequent bombing of
my home town, I had heard thousands, and I advised him to
have the barrack-rooms' and street lights in that huge area
put out. The Indian in charge of the barracks power station
refused our repeated attempts to have this done but when I
finally explained to him that the planes we could hear were
Japanese and that they were approaching his station with
bombs, the lights were out before the phone was on its rest!

On that same day, of course, the very much greater attack
was made on the American base at Pearl Harbour where their
Far Eastern Fleet was reduced to scrap metal and many
lives were lost. No declaration of war was made by Japan,

who relied on the well-known capacity of armies the world over to sleep off Saturday's binge on Sunday morning, and to a surprise attack at that hour on Sunday to catch the enemy off his guard. However, it should be remembered that a Far Eastern war had been expected for months, a massive Japanese convoy with naval and aerial escorts had been spotted in the South China Sea, and that when the British-loaned radar operator had reported both the earlier feint attack and the later committed one, he had been told to 'go back to bed'. So are wars started, lost and won.

If any comfort was to be found that day it was that the *Prince of Wales* and the *Repulse* had been anchored at the naval base. (I had seen the former leave the Tyne in the late twenties, and a magnificent concentration of strength and grace she was). Two days later, 10 December 1941, the two capital ships left the naval base, unescorted either aerially or nautically, for the South China Sea, with the intention of denying the Japanese any further use of Singora, on the Siam/Malaya littoral, for the landing of troops and material. It is reported that on breaking free of the sea mist, Admiral Tom Phillips realised that when no escorts were available, his ships were sitting ducks and he turned south again into the mist. Realising that no war could be fought by such methods, he once again turned north, and as he emerged into the sunshine he was attacked by aerial torpedoes. The two ships were soon crippled, their electric circuits destroyed, and their guns being manhandled into position by their crews. In two hours all was lost, and both ships disappeared with appalling loss of life. In true Royal Naval tradition they sank with their guns firing, and their admiral standing at the salute as they keeled over. In forty-eight hours virtually all allied naval presence had been eliminated from South East Asia!

Nor were the reports from the north of the Malayan Peninsula any more encouraging. Even allowing for the fact that the attacking force has a tactical advantage it was apparent that the advance was not being stemmed. The Japs were racing for Kota Bahru under an aerial umbrella, and the inadequacies of our own aerial defences were quickly demonstrated. It was reported that the Japanese literally 'flew rings around' them and the gallantry of our crews merely ensured them an early death. Instead of running for home they stayed to be shot down at will, and within hours we had no effective RAF, either for operations against their convoy and supply lines or directly against their advancing army.

It is an axiom of war that the longer your supply lines the more vulnerable you are, and to a great extent Command appeared to rely on this as a handicap to the Japanese. However, two things militated against this: we had no air capability, and because the Japanese were advancing down a narrow peninsula they could both supply and reinforce their armies, from the South China Sea as well as from the Indian Ocean; and this they did throughout the campaign.

As operations moved closer so aerial attacks on the island increased, and despite courageous stands at various points on the mainland it soon seemed inevitable that the Japanese would be able to attack the island in great force. As our sea-borne supplies were now being denied to us, and investing of the island was a distinct possibility in the near future, I advised our Chinese typist, Lee Choon Eng, to give up his employment and – if the worst should happen – never to admit to the Japanese that he had been in army employment. (Chia Soo Hiang had been employed by the Inspector General of Police since the previous November, so he was no longer my problem).

By mid-January 1942 more and more troops and civilians and their transport were coming onto the island from Malaya, and the streets were a vast carpark. Many of the civilians, particularly women and children, were able to leave for overseas destinations by sea, but such journeys, usually commenced in the hours of darkness, were hazardous in the extreme, and those unlucky enough to have their transports sunk were usually bombed and machine-gunned in the water by the Japanese.

On Sunday 8 February a violent explosion indicated that the causeway joining the mainland to the island had been breached by our troops, indicating that we no longer had a presence in Malaya. The 'Island Fortress of Singapore' was now approaching its end as the main bastion of British defence in the Far East. Hong Kong had fallen to the Japanese on Christmas Day, 1941, a dreadful portent of what was to occur in so many places in the next few months; Borneo, New Guinea, Celebes, Java, Sumatra, Bali, – virtually all the territories of the British and Dutch Far Eastern colonial empires – an old sovereignty that was to be replaced by something so barbarous and obscene that even now the world does not fully comprehend it, and its perpetrators attempt to re-write history in order that its foulness may at least be unknown to its future population.

Within two days we were evacuated from Alexandra Barracks on the west side of the island, because of the advance of the Japanese infantry, a wise precaution as those same troops occupied Alexandra Military Hospital and murdered by bayonet and bullet the totally unarmed nurses, consultants and patients, including those anaesthetized on the operating table and those wounded in the fighting.

We moved to attap huts in River Valley Road and there a call was made for volunteers to take our only two Lewis guns and man the area on which the Japs were expected to make their next attack. Four of us stepped forward (I had recently completed a Lewis gun course), we were made up into pairs of one NCO and one OR, each pair being issued with one gun and two pans of ammunition, two rifles with a hundred rounds each, two Mills bombs and one loaded revolver. We two were taken to a crossroads a mile away and there, having built a sandbagged defence around a monsoon ditch, we made our stand. We could hear fairly heavy machine-gun fire just over the hill ahead of us, we were constantly harassed by a sniper whose location we never traced, and heavy shelling and bombing continued, as it did throughout that entire last week. We stayed there for twenty-four hours without food or water and without engaging the enemy. At the end of that time I stopped a dispatch rider and asked him to contact my unit. We were eventually collected by a thirty-hundredweight truck and returned to unit, where it was admitted that they had completely forgotten us. A more likely explanation was forthcoming when it transpired that we had been written off because of the intensity of the fighting.

Because of the shortage of doctors I was asked by Colonel Pope to set up a small casualty clearing station on the following day when we had moved to a private house nearer the city. I was given a room, twelve canvas stretchers and a pathetically limited supply of antiseptics and dressings. However, I was informed that there was an evacuated GP's surgery nearby that the natives were looting. I had no sooner arrived, feeling much like a thief, when I was joined by a captain in army uniform to whom I remarked how grateful I was that the owner of the flat couldn't see his property in this state; to which he replied, 'He can, it's mine'. When I explained my mission, he invited me to take everything I wanted as he was leaving permanently. With my stock thus replenished in dressings, antiseptics and a few surgical instruments I was able to provide a much better service.

The hell of that week is unlikely to be forgotten by anyone who experienced it: perpetual shelling and bombing, aerial machine-gunning, sniper fire (I reported him to a patrolling brigadier who took a small detachment and shot him out of a tree a hundred yards away), the cat-naps of total exhaustion, the constant supply of wounded men, and the prospect of final captivity combined to make it the worst week of anyone's life, a view held even by men who had been through the Dunkirk evacuation. Corpses littered the streets of Singapore, large numbers of buildings were destroyed, and a vast umbrella of black smoke overhung the island from the various burning oil depots. This was mainly due to our denial policy as the enemy would certainly have conserved such stocks.

On 11 February I spent seven hours on wounds of various sorts – dispatch riders blown off motor cycles, minor battle casualties, and so forth, and went onto the balcony of the house after I had discharged my last patient. Within minutes I heard a shell which seemed to be coming my way. I fell flat, and the shell exploded on my medical room and totally destroyed it, along with my personal kit. I salvaged what I could of dressings, scissors, and other equipment, and my appeal to the men for their field dressings was generously answered.

On Black Friday, 13 February, we moved to St Nicholas' Flats. In the late afternoon I was ordered by my late adjutant Major Robert Peel, to muster as many men as possible from Fortress Signals, as they were to proceed overseas as a signals unit. They were all in outlying houses, a blackout was in force and shelling was continuing. I therefore detailed them very much as I found them, without regard to rank or trade. Within hours they were all dead, the destroyer on which they left the island being lost shortly after getting out to sea. To this day I feel a degree of responsibility for their deaths. I knew all of them and several were close friends.

Owing to the bombing and shelling, the Pierce and MacRitchie reservoirs on the island had lost their ability to send water to us, presumably because the conduits had been destroyed. In view of our proximity to the Equator this merely added a further obstacle to our capacity to continue fighting. Whatever supply lines had met our needs from India and home had long since been severed, and most of the crews had gone to Davy Jones' locker with their ships. In early February I watched the sister ship to the *Empress of Japan*, the *Empress of Asia*, ablaze in Singapore roads as a result of Japanese bombing, and her troops and crew who survived the attack leaving the vessel by any means – diving from the deck, through portholes or being thrown into the sea by non-injured comrades.

On 12 February I received Christmas and New Year cables from my parents sent on 10 December 1941. They were to be my last communications of an up-to-date nature with anyone at home for three years and eight months.

The end was now as obvious as it was inevitable. On Sunday 15 February 1942 our GOC, General Percival, set out under a flag of truce to meet General Yamashita, the Tiger of Malaya, at the Ford factory at Bukit Timah. He was intercepted by a detachment of Royal Northumberland Fusiliers whose major refused to allow Percival to proceed under a white flag. He relented only when his colonel had been found and ordered him to withdraw. The unfortunate outcome of this was that Yamashita, suffering a severe loss of face, smashed a lignum vitae ruler across Percival's face, thus introducing the British garrison to the first of many barbarities and obscenities that were to be inflicted throughout occupied Asia in the succeeding years.

We spent the greater part of that day in a denial

procedure, destroying signals equipment, vehicles and stores that might be of use to the enemy. As the Japanese were reputed to become violently mad under the influence of alcohol, I was ordered to destroy all stocks; and I spent the better part of two hours dispatching whisky, brandy, gin, port and sherry down a drain.

At 9 pm the guns fell silent for the first time for days, the 'Island Fortress' of Singapore capitulated and became, instead, Syonan, a colony of the Japanese Empire.

It is foolish to speculate now on the causes of that failure. The products of many rain-forests have provided paper for innumerable treatises on that subject. Two things are certain: without a European war in progress Japan would never have attacked the British Empire; and having attacked the USA at Pearl Harbour, Japan had confirmed her own eventual defeat with the first salvo, so great was the American potential for retaliation. In the event, that retaliation was the most cataclysmic horror that the world had witnessed.

Statistical fact and wartime propaganda have clashed in their statements on the number of British personnel taken prisoner in this greatest defeat of British arms. In order, I think, to impress the Australians, a figure as high as 110,000 was given at that time. Those present in Singapore talked in terms of 68,000, and this still seems to be near the truth.

3

Orders were issued by the Imperial Japanese Army that all POWs were to be over the Tampines Road, Changi, by 1830 hours on Tuesday, 17 February, and anyone arriving after that time would be shot. Sparse transport would be provided only for the severely wounded or acutely sick, and all other personnel were to march the eighteen miles to Changi Barracks, carrying all their possessions.

In view of the nearness of the campaign, the presence of many light sick and the temperature, I was asked by Colonel Pope if I would continue with my medical bag. This would involve leaving the city last of all as I was expected to collect those who had fallen by the wayside en route. The Japanese had promised that I would be provided with a lorry for this purpose.

By mid-morning I had said goodbye to all my cobbers, and sat back to await my lorry. At 1300 hours it was my double misfortune to be joined by Lieutenant G. and to be told by him that the promise of the lorry had been withdrawn and that I was to walk. I suggested to him that it would serve my patients', and his and my purpose, if I purloined the biggest vehicle I could find and we drove to Changi in style. He was panic-stricken at my suggestion and forbade any such action, mainly through fear of the Japanese response if we were caught.

So we marched through the debris, the death and desolation of that once-great city. As the afternoon advanced we became increasingly dehydrated and hungry, and on the appearance of an ambulance from the rear I showed my Red Cross brassard and asked if he would take G. and me to Tampines cross-roads, and he readily agreed.

G. was less than pleased when I told him that I had no intention of crossing the line into captivity before 1829 hours. I spent my time in washing in a nearby stream, cleaning my teeth, smoking and reading.

At about 1800 hours a car driven by a Japanese soldier pulled up and from it stepped a senior officer resplendent in silk shirt, green jacket, riding breeches and boots. He indicated my gold watch and ring, presents from my fiancée, and in the international 'gimme' signal held out his open hand. I very emphatically refused to hand them over. This enraged him to such an extent that he began to shout his demands, to which I responded with equal vociferation. He then resorted to the Malayan language, and I replied in kind. He retired defeated but in a matter of weeks I realised how near my obstinacy had brought me to an untimely end.

Captors have all the rights, captives, particularly where the Japanese are concerned, none.

And so we 'crossed over on to the other side'. We were less than comforted by the knowledge that four years before, the Japanese had murdered 300,000 in the Rape of Nanking and this had involved the violation of many thousands of young women, looting and partial destruction of the city, and the torture and execution of all who stood in their way. It was a scenario that was to be repeated throughout South East Asia ad nauseam in the succeeding three and a half years.

It blasphemes God to refer to such creatures as part of the divine creation.

4

CAPTIVITY – II

The Japanese denied any of the humanities to their service and civilian captives by the simple and truthful expedient of stating that they did not now uphold the Geneva Convention. They saw this as a license to inflict whatever suffering they liked on us, and this included the virtual total absence of any medical aid – despite the cornucopia of all forms of medical and surgical equipment stored by the British against just such a contingency, and a well-organised hospital service throughout the island and peninsula – starvation, torture, execution, hard labour, the withholding or destruction of correspondence, and employment of captives on military enterprises, i.e., construction of gun-emplacements, trenches, manning of equipment, etc.

The problem of any autobiography such as this is that one may be accused of exaggeration by those who never experienced the 1939–45 war or who imagine that they serve the causes of peace and full employment by apologising for the Japanese. I can only say that I have recorded events as factually and accurately as possible. Where they concern me I have presented them as representative of an overall picture, not as an attempt to gain sympathy, but as an indication of a general pattern.

I also rely heavily on a wealth of previously recorded chronicles to give verisimilitude to an epoch which the Japanese are now seeking to deny. Whether this is due to a spirit of atonement or to industrial and financial expansion it is up to the world to decide.

Changi Barracks followed the pattern of all such establishments in India, Ceylon and South-East Asia: spacious, three-storey buildings complete with toilets and showers, extensive flower-gardens and lawns, and all the ancillary services of catering, electricity, entertainments etc. Under British rule, Chinese civilians did the clerical work, and preparation and cooking of food, under the supervision of service personnel; and gardening and sanitation were usually provided by the Tamil population. Laundry work was contracted out on a weekly basis to 'Dhobi wallahs', Chinese women were allowed into barracks for clothing repairs, and Indians shaved and gave haircuts, were employed on a permanent basis as 'boys' to provide morning and afternoon tea, polish shoes and brasses, make beds, raise and lower mosquito nets, and do individual shopping. This gives the traditional picture of the Raj leading an easy life in the Empire but it had the twin virtues of allowing the serviceman to get on with his work and of creating a great deal of employment for the local population.

Changi is on the eastern edge of the island, has an extensive littoral with bathing pagars and palm trees and sunny beaches, and a view of Penggerang, Johore and the South China Sea. I am told that the barracks were built to accommodate 2,000.

So of course we were now faced with a quart into a pint-pot situation. How to get 68,000 people, many of them ill but fortunately all of the same sex, into a series of buildings most of which had received major damage from the bombs and shells and to which no water supplies existed. We didn't 'double-up', of course: we quadrupled and quintupled-up. We slept under huts and out in the open. One must remember that the island of Singapore is given to frequent flash rainstorms of a monsoon nature, and when these are accompanied by a Sumatra wind the results are frequently disastrous. In such circumstances there are no alternatives to a bit of stoicism and sticking it out.

To be fair to the Japanese one has to admit that, even if they had wished to, they had little opportunity in less than forty-eight hours to make any provision for our two greatest needs: food and toilets. So far as food is concerned, the

33

Japanese can squat down with a mess-tin, some water and a handful of rice over a fire and they have, at least, a hunger-inhibiting meal in a short time. Tommy Atkins and the erks and matelots of the other services enjoy no such facilities. We attempted to put to good use a British Field Service stove, an ideal instrument for providing stews of meat and vegetables, but totally disastrous as a means of cooking our first issue of rice. This experiment produced a soggy, glutinous, and totally inedible lump that would have defeated an eupeptic elephant. On that day we had a total food consumption of four biscuits, each about two and a half inches in diameter. Sufficient latrines had been dug to meet our immediate needs; and there was some semblance of an attempt to organise cooking facilities, even though the proximity of al fresco cooking to latrines provided the foundation of a shattering amoebic and bacillary dysentery epidemic that was to last for months and kill several hundred people.

From the outset it was apparent that we were to have no culinary luxuries: what we didn't realise was that the poor standard we had then could deteriorate so much in the following years. As with potatoes, rice has a poor nutritional level, and the poorer the quality of the rice, the lower the nutrient. Throughout captivity we had the broken small-grain rice grown locally, a high proportion of whose content consisted of rats' droppings (and, by association, their urine), maggots and weevils. The more fastidious of us spent a considerable part of those early days in picking out the foreign bodies but we soon realised that we were removing about ten per cent of the bulk, and in any case the pressure of time when on working parties precluded such finesse. So we ate the lot, with considerable revulsion, and without salt, pepper or sugar.

An interesting sideline on this was a notice, which I saw with my own eyes (how else), typed and on the unit door, which recommended that if the rice were placed on a sheet of newspaper, the maggots and weevils would crawl underneath and the newspaper could then be lifted up and the rice cooked: BUT attention was drawn to the fact that such creatures would provide an essential dietary supplement in the form of protein! Even accepting that recommendation, how and where in a POW camp holding 68,000 does one obtain the newspaper to contain the rice for three meals a day? I suppose one must be grateful in retrospect that even in our most unoptimistic moments we never imagined that our incarceration would last for three and a half years, and that we would eat almost 4,000 meals of rice in that time. It would be wrong to pretend that we didn't on occasion have additions by the way of pumpkin stew, seaweed and even meat but the basic meal was always and ineluctably rice.

I had always had the greatest respect for my CO, Colonel F.T. Pope, and when he invited me through my RSM to continue with my medical work I was happy to agree, the more so as this was never issued as an order. However, it was impossible for reasons of weather and hygiene to hold out-patient sessions by my open-air bed-space under a hut, and the sole condition I made was that I should occupy the NCO's small accommodation at the end of the hut. This was reluctantly accepted, and I moved in with my small supplies of drugs and equipment. The RSM entered the legend on the end of the hut, in chalk:

'DR G.F. KERSHAW, CONSULTANT,
O.P. SESSIONS DAILY 08.30–1200; 1400–1700.
PREGNANCIES BY SPECIAL APPT.'

One of the rewards of the post-war years lies in the number of people who have stopped to thank me for those efforts, including a Chelsea Pensioner who stopped me in the Festival Hall in 1985, and showed me his neatly-healed wound. He was probably almost ninety.

It wasn't long before I was called out during the night, sometimes on several occasions, but these were mainly to dysentery cases who were in severe abdominal pain and bleeding profusely, rectally. Until the Japanese occupied the island it had been malaria-free but many of the troops had been up-country and had contracted the disease there. I soon learned to recognise the high temperature and associated headache, and with both these diagnoses my only course lay in making the patients as comfortable as possible and referring them to Roberts Hospital the following day by stretcher or hand-pulled lorry.

At this time it seemed a shame to me that I should have spare accommodation and that my closest friend, Frank Pidgeon, should still be 'under the hut'. Knowing the army's way of thinking, I suggested to the RSM, with some trepidation, that Frank should join me. As anticipated, the problem of homosexuality immediately reared its head. It was implicit rather than explicit, and buttressed by the fact that I was an NCO. I told the RSM that he and we had worked closely together for almost a year and that this was hardly the time to quote King's Regulations. Permission was eventually granted and I look upon that period as one of the happier parts of the incarceration. Unfortunately it was to last less than a month.

We continued to be woefully short of water, both for consumption and hygiene, and long queues formed in order to obtain even a mess-tin full from a trickling tap. The heat and humidity of Singapore worsened the situation very considerably, of course, so we took to the bathing pagar whenever possible. We could at least scrub ourselves with sand in the interests of hygiene. As soon as the Japanese realised how much we enjoyed this it was stopped, with the threat of dire punishment for infringement.

For the first few weeks we were issued with ten cigarettes per week. We normally kept these until Saturday night when those of us who were music-lovers assembled in D Block, sat on horizontal metal lockers, and listened to music ground out on a portable gramophone with metal needles or a honky-tonk ex-NAAFI piano. To this day I never hear the most popular piece, Dvorak's *New World Symphony*, without a thought for those who shared those sessions with me, most of whom died on the Death Railway or in other places of Japanese destruction in the following years.

Within days I was visited by DADMS (Deputy Assistant Director of Medical Services) to discuss the situation from a medical viewpoint. I showed him what I was trying to do from one small room about ten feet by six feet. He immediately ordered that a hut should be put at my disposal (I think it had been standing empty and locked for some time), and sent me two dozen stretchers and blankets.

36

I regret to say that many of these stretchers were occupied by men who had a total anorexia for rice, and to whom no persuasion was plausible. I couldn't refer them to Robert's Hospital (within Changi Camp), as the raging dysentery epidemic there would inevitably have involved them. As no food other than rice was available my only contribution lay in making them as comfortable as possible until death supervened. It was an appalling waste as most of them were healthy men. DADMS continued to visit me at regular intervals, honoured his promise to supply me with whatever was available, and expressed himself satisfied with all that he found.

As has already been noted, the proximity of cooking areas to latrines, and the migration between the two of millions of blue-bottles quickly resulted in endemic amoebic and bacillary dysentery, the former usually and the latter frequently resulting in extremely painful death. As with most of our illnesses the means to treat them existed in abundance in the godowns of Singapore, but the Japanese refused to issue other than the very minimum of simple treatment, and Epsom salts is no therapy for such illnesses. Part of the main barracks was quickly converted to Roberts Hospital and was soon overflowing with 3,000 patients and an enormous mortality rate.

The lack of drugs was compounded by lack of water, and affected patients in four ways:

(1) There was no means of combatting the dehydration caused by fever and climate.
(2) Personal hygiene either for patients or orderlies was non-existent.
(3) There were no flush toilets. Open containers as previously used on the coolie lines were employed and were usually overflowing and infested with flies.
(4) Incontinence on the wards was frequent and as the floor was of concrete could easily have been swilled away. Instead it dried very quickly and was dispersed overall in dust storms.

The nearness of the Equator meant that it was dark from about 1800 hours to 0600 hours, and everything had to be done by Braille – feeding, attending to the sick, emptying latrine containers, and removing the dead. All had to be done in Stygian darkness.

At the outset of the epidemic we attempted to give a normal burial, and our captors even provided one or two boxwood coffins. The Last Post and Reveille were bugled on each occasion, but as the mortality rate increased it cast an enormous gloom over the camp, so much so that our captors finally ordered the cessation of all ceremony.

About this time, end of February, the Japanese ordered that *all* personnel were to parade for special occasions, the only exceptions being those who were too ill to walk. As the parade involved some top brass, thought to be Tojo, we were to bow as he passed. The very thought of making obeisance to such a creature revolted me, and I refused to go, thus being the only healthy person not on the parade. In the light of subsequent experience it was probably a foolhardy act, as I should undoubtedly have been bayonetted to death for insulting the Imperial Japanese Army, but I got enormous satisfaction from my obstinacy!

By the second week in March Nemesis had overtaken me. I began to have severe abdominal pains and diarrhoea with the passing of the usual large quantities of blood on each occasion. The frequency became so great that eventually I took my groundsheet and sat for hours at a time on an open-air thunder-box. By 18 March I had lost both a great deal of weight and the use of my left leg from the hip, and I was transported to hospital by stretcher, a two-hour journey on foot undertaken by friends in blazing sunshine.

All that we had heard of this modern Scutari was now abundantly confirmed: no running water, no toilets, no electricity, a totally inadequate diet, beds so closely packed that it was almost impossible to get to and from one's bed (a major problem when incontinence frequently threatened), both wet and dry faeces invariably on the floor and a drug supply that seemed to consist only of Epsom salts – by kind permission of our inhuman captors. It goes without saying that the luxuries of toilet paper and soap (the latter to be used with one mess-tin of water), were as conspicuously absent as were the blue-bottles conspicuously present, in profusion. The only advantage, particularly with high personal and weather temperatures, was that the huge doors on both sides and ends of the wards could be opened for ventilation, but the humidity in Singapore is so high at most times that it did little more than help to clear the appalling smell. We could at least claim to be the largest hospital in the world with over 3,000 patients, and to have the highest turnover in the world thanks to an unparalleled morbidity and mortality but I think that poor old Hippocrates must have shed many a tear on our behalf. By dawn one's friends of the previous night had gone to greater glory and their beds had been occupied by the new intake; at least the orderlies were spared the task of changing the bed-linen, as none existed.

It would be impossible to pay too high a tribute to the medical officers and orderlies of the RAMC in such appalling circumstances. Their devotion and compassion ensured that whatever could be done to encourage survival or ease the crossing to the other side was performed without stint, and many paid for it with their lives.

Probably 90 per cent of the doctors who came to the Far East from Britain had only the basic medical qualifications of baccalaureateships in medicine and surgery, and only a transient acquaintance from student days with malaria, cholera, dysentery and beriberi. In pre-war days there was virtually no high-speed international travel, and the greatest carriers of tropical diseases – liners and troopships – were well-equipped with drugs and suitably-qualified doctors to handle such diseases.

Many of our service doctors were denied the opportunity to advance their knowledge on arrival by visiting hospitals and medical school, because fighting was imminent or had already commenced, and as the campaign lasted only sixty-nine days even those in the base camps were kept fully occupied with casualties.

It was bad enough that they should be faced with bomb-damaged buildings without water-supply at the completion of the short but violent campaign, but to be faced with a series of endemic diseases on such a vast scale, for which no clinical facilities were permitted by the Japanese, made life impossible for both doctor and patient alike. Pathological and radiological facilities were also non-existent in the immediate area; thus all diagnoses were concluded on the basis of physical examination of the patient and macroscopic examination of stools, a highly-empirical process when the doctor wasn't quite sure what he was looking for, or indeed, what the treatment should be once the diagnosis was made! The results of such a hitty-missy approach could be seen in the morbidity and mortality of the various doctors involved, and they varied widely.

The prognoses of many of these same doctors were equally gloomy; it was confidently forecast that our gums would overgrow our teeth through lack of solid food, that our teeth, once covered, would rot away, and that we should all become sterile. The post-war reproductive processes of those who returned hardly support such a prediction, I am glad to say!

It was my great good fortune to be admitted to the care of Captain Scott, a Canadian of enormous competence and charm, a student of Urdu, and the possessor of a most profound compassion. Despite what must have been the most apppalling burden he was ever likely to meet professionally, he examined in detail, listened with enthusiasm and discussed with sympathy each patient's case, where that was possible. There were no medical records as we weren't allowed paper, no X-ray and pathology reports as such services didn't exist, and routine temperature-taking appeared to be a confidence that the orderly kept strictly to himself – apart from an occasional reference to the MO.

My diary records that I was given only magnesium sulphate for three days with small doses of chlorodyne and opium to relieve the pain, and that my only intake was of watered tinned soup, milk and Bovril from 18 to 30 March 1942. As a means of passing time I recorded the number of times I went to the toilet, and even for those times the total of 320 calls in four days must have qualified me for the Guinness Book of Records. Without going into too many details it may be sufficient to record that I continued in such painful bleeding for so long that I eventually passed into delirium for long periods, and eventually awoke as a totally unidentifiable figure of sunken eyes and cheeks, large beard and almost total loss of soft tissue. I was then six stones – from thirteen stones on 18 March.

My left thigh and leg were now causing as much concern as the dysentery. All power and sensation had long since gone, and I was able to struggle to the toilet only with the support of the intervening beds, a process that earned me many a hard word from the sleeping occupants; no such things as crutches and sticks were available, of course. The condition was now diagnosed as one of the earliest cases of beriberi, and a consultant was called in to confirm this. He immediately accused me of being an alcoholic, and when I assured him that in fifteen months since I had left England I had had probably no more than six pints of beer and three small whiskies, he told me that he didn't believe me. I replied that there were several people in the ward who would confirm that I was something of a joke where alcohol consumption was concerned but he was unconvinced.

He told me to close my eyes and tell him when I felt anything. As I made no response after two minutes he told me to see what had happened and I found about twelve places from my thigh to great toe which were bleeding where he had stuck an unsterilised safety-pin very deeply. He then confirmed that I had beriberi in my leg, eyes and possibly my left lung. I am grateful to record that I never saw him again. As a result of this diagnosis I was given one level dessert-spoonful of Marmite four times a day, which skinned my mouth and set my heart pounding, but at least it gave me some vitamins.

On 16 April, 1942, after two months of captivity, the water supply was restored from 0001 hours to 0900 hours daily; at least we could now wash, and clean the ward occasionally. On 22 April I had my first tentative walk for five weeks but the reaction was so bad that I was forbidden such folly, except to the end of the ward. At least I was now slowly regaining the use of my leg. On 9 May a patient went mad at 0530 and jumped off a twenty-five foot high verandah, bruised himself severely, and died of dysentery the following day.

The death rate continued unabated, which wasn't surprising in view of all the problems of hygiene, drugs, climate and food. On 15 May we had a Lucullan banquet of boiled peanuts and rice, the latter in ever-smaller amounts as the Imperial Japanese Army apparently thought we were gourmandising, but still generously provided with maggots and weevils.

I volunteered on 11 May to resume my medical duties. The orderlies were under continuous pressure, I was becoming increasingly bored (a good sign), and I felt that the exercise would help my leg. I issued Epsom salts, covered wounds with improvised dressings, and issued meals. Strenuous but rewarding; my dysentery had almost disappeared, my eyes were improving and my weight was now over nine stones.

On 15 June after three months in hospital I was discharged to unit with a written request that I should be given only light duties. With its usual sympathetic indulgence this was interpreted to mean the same as the others were doing – and I was soon drilling boreholes, wood-chopping and pulling the ration lorry. On 17 July I was taken off this work as my heart problems had returned and I was losing visual accommodation, both due to beriberi.

When the Japanese overran the Far East in 1942 they designated the entire invested area The Greater East-Asia Co-prosperity Sphere. It was a joke of the most distorted and macabre kind, and many of the natives from the former colonies of Britain and Holland, eager to welcome the invaders with their promise of 'liberation', were soon praying for the return of their former 'captors'. Wherever the Imperial Japanese Army set its feet it instituted a system of torture, execution, robbery and rape. In Singapore, huge numbers of Chinese were tied together, forced to jump into the harbour, and were then machine-gunned for no other reason than their nationality. Few people will forget the Chinese who were tied to the railings in Singapore, kept without food or water in the tropical heat, and fitted with a barbed wire crown of thorns. It was the duty of each soldier who passed to lift the crown and crash it down on the torn and bleeding head; and no Jap soldier ever forwent the opportunity. How gratefully those coolies accepted death!

From both the military and civilian viewpoints the continuing raping and robbery of all the territories occupied by the Japanese served only to underwrite their contempt for their victims, and their arrogant conviction that they were invincible and the outcome of the war never in doubt. What they had committed themselves to many years before – war throughout the Far East, with eyes particularly turned towards India, Malaya and the Dutch East Indies – had seemed more feasible by 1941 than even their most optimistic assessments of the past decade.

The hugely-successful investment of so much of Europe by Germany, the elimination of France from the war, and the rapid advance of panzers and infantry across Russia presented the Japanese government with an opportunity to fulfil all her ambitions with equal speed. Those members of the government who had opposed war had been easily eliminated, and a belligerent and committed war cabinet had been created.

Had its members been more given to assessment of the military potential of its enemies and less dazzled by the glittering prizes that were there for the apparent taking they would have realised that by attacking the American Pacific Fleet at Pearl Harbour they declared war not only on that country but also on the British Empire, the Dutch Empire and Russia.

With equal foresight in another direction they might have realised that, by cultivating the goodwill of the various native populations, and taking advantage of the disaffection felt by many of them towards their erstwhile colonial masters, they would have had a ready-made army in every territory to repel every attempt by those same masters to return; and in addition they would have had a team of competent administrators and other professionals to advance the Japanese cause.

In the event, exactly the opposite was the case, and in the majority of areas the former authorities were welcomed with open arms at the end of the war.

In pursuit of this process of intimidation the Japanese now insisted that military personnel should individually sign forms stating that if they attempted to escape and were caught they would be shot. This was strenuously resisted by our senior officers, despite the threat of dire results, and on 2 September 1942 the Japanese ordered that all personnel in Changi, except hospital patients and essential staff, should move to Selerang Barracks as punishment.

Selerang, three miles from Changi, was built for one battalion (about 600 men), and into it the Japanese crowded 15,400 officers and men. Our captors were only too well aware that a repetition of the Changi epidemic was inevitable, as open latrines had to be dug, there was only space for one, adjacent, cooking area, and thousands of men were living in the open without hope of shelter and with even less food. By the third day the Japanese threatened to move in the entire hospital from Changi, with the inevitable rise in the incidence of disease and death. Faced with such odds by an inhuman foe the senior officers gave in; with only one tap, starvation, disease and the threat to use machine-guns which had been mounted at several points, it was the only sensible course to take, with duress as the over-riding reason. Thus to Scutari we had now added our own Black Hole of Calcutta. I am grateful that my absence from Changi camp at that time allows me to record the story only objectively: I merely signed the resultant form.

I mentioned earlier that we lived virtually exclusively on 'manure' rice (so called because that grade of rice is frequently used as fertiliser by coolie farmers), but like all such generalisations it has to be qualified. I completely forgot the issue of Vitameal, made and bagged in Lancashire in 1929 and clearly so marked on the hessian bags. It was, of course, pig food, generously endowed with weevils and maggots, but much tastier and more nutritious than the rice. When the final issue was made a week or two later there was almost a riot but many people felt significantly better for the improved diet.

Frank Pidgeon had continued to visit me in hospital during my three-months-long stay, even though on the first occasion he had failed to recognise me with my beard, moustache and severe loss of weight, and on my discharge to unit we continued our sturdy friendship. In such circumstances the presence of a supportive confidant is worth even more than in freedom, and we buttressed each other's moods and needs as much as possible. We attended the 'concerts' in D Block on Saturdays, dressed in shirts and slacks, and carrying our carefully-hoarded issue of ten cigarettes, talked endlessly of our families and post-war plans, and discussed the English language, books, music, and, inevitably in those circumstances, food and menus.

Then suddenly that part of our lives ended when I was detailed to join the other white coolies in Singapore and Frank's name wasn't on the roster. On 2 August 1942, I was sitting on the lorry when Frank asked if I had a blanket. When I answered that I hadn't he told me that he had two, rushed indoors and brought one to me. In those circumstances it was an act of supreme generosity as he could have kept it for himself in view of our indeterminable stay or sold it for many dollars in order to buy precious food. As Frank never left the island while captive he is still unaware of the enormous benefits of his gift: it was a matter of honour in the jungle camps of Siam to pile all available blankets on those suffering from malarial rigors, and in the bitter cold and sodden conditions of the monsoon night it brought a comfort known only to those who have experienced it: a slice of heaven in a monotonous hell.

From earliest days Changi had been split into compounds, presumably for security reasons, and it was possible to pass between compounds only with a Japanese escort. Our new domicile was the Great World, one of three such centres on the island, the others being the New and Happy Worlds. In happier days it had been the focus of cheap entertainment – taxi dancers (they covered a multitude of sins), alcohol, stage shows and good food, mainly of the Chinese variety. The huge dining and dancing area with its concrete floor had been cleared and the entire floor covered with trestle tables of a most insecure kind as many of the screws in the hinges were slack or had fallen out. Furthermore the table-tops were saturated with dried blood as they had been used as the last resting-place for many of the people afflicted by the Japanese bombing and shelling. Even if we had had the facilities and permission it would have been impossible to remove this as it was congealed in large lumps both on top and in the interstices of the planks. The tables were so adjacent, one foot space to each three beds, that it was almost impossible to pass between them, and the Stygian gloom of the whole hall, containing several hundred men, was relieved only by one very low-watt bulb.

The Japanese referred to us as cattle, and they were determined to treat us as such; and this was never more apparent than on the first night when we discovered that each table was host to several hundred bed-bugs who greeted us with ravenous enthusiasm. We never eliminated them.

Our daily labours now brought us into much closer contact with the Japanese, and we began to see them as the louts and bullies that subsequent events proved them to be throughout South East Asia. To be just, it must be noted that they appeared to be entirely of the labouring class, both illiterate and innumerate, and in striking contrast to the Imperial Guards with whom we had previously come in contact. As with the majority of that race their average height was considerably below ours but they possessed the guns, bayonets, boots and fists, and the authority to deal with us by any means they thought fit if we defended ourselves, an authority that they never ceased to employ. I suppose it was an understandable reaction; the Japanese underdog had destroyed the British Empire in the Far East and had become the heroes of the motherland.

Our duties were many and varied: we stacked 224 pound bags of rice single-handed, (ten bags to a ton, and back-breaking when a height of twenty feet had to be climbed to the top of the godown), each bag being held together by ropes with a central knot. When the Japanese helped to lift the bag to shoulder level they delighted in banging it down on the recipient and then gouging the knot into one's sweating back. It wasn't very long before a most satisfactory wound could be created in several backs, to say nothing of the severe muscular pain in the lower spine.

We built brick walls in Singapore Cold Storage for the preparation of vegetables, spent eight hours per day in godown refrigerators in ankle-deep iced water, moving sides of meat and sorting rotten vegetables and fish. At least when we dumped the result outside we were able to conceal generous amounts of good food for the starving local population who swarmed on us and almost tore us from the lorries. (Thanks to the Japanese habit of constructing almost all their words on consonant-vowel repetition, and usually ending with a vowel, we were totally deceived one day when the Japanese soldier promised that when we finished our eight-hour stint in the refrigerator there would be 'all the men – cocoa'. We rubbed our frozen hands in anticipatory glee, only to find when we got outside that we had five tons of coke to move!)

We usually marched to these assignments, and one route took us past a working party of Gurkhas, those wonderful and loyal Nepalese soldiers who had done such splendid work with their machine-guns and kukris against the Japanese military in the campaign. As with all such personnel they came to rigid attention and saluted the officer in charge. I am deeply ashamed to say that one officer, a 'made-up' regular, was always looking the other way and refused to return the salute. As a result, it was a point of honour for any NCO to return the salute, with suitable loud comments about the cowardice of the officer, which never had any effect. On one such occasion, when two parties were working adjacently, a Gurkha soldier who spoke excellent English told me that each day, in an effort to persuade them to defect, the Japanese were selecting one Gurkha at random and shooting him if he refused to defect. He asked for my advice because their loyalty to the King Emperor was being severely tested. I advised him that they should defect in a body, as when we had won the war the King Emperor would understand and forgive because of such severe duress, and they would live to fight again. I never knew the outcome as I left the island shortly afterwards.

We were now working with ex-British food stocks, and the Japanese in their abundant generosity occasionally gave us one small tin of baked beans for every ten or fifteen men, depending on the size of the working party. There were dire punishments for pilfering, of course, and many men were beaten almost to death for augmenting their diet with tinned food. On one occasion this presented me with a serious problem. As the work was light but risky I had taken the medical bag, and as things were quiet I was detailed to cook the rice. The cookhouse was one previously used by coolies and was brick built with four vents for the cans. I put the usual five-gallon petrol tins on the four fireplaces, added the rice and water and lit the fires. One of my friends then came in with a leg of pork which he had purloined from the refrigerator, said 'Put that in the rice' and disappeared. As I had no knife I had no means of preparing or dicing it, and simply put it untouched into the third tin. After half an hour there was a wonderful aroma of pork filling the tiny hut, when I saw to my horror a Japanese officer heading my way with three privates. I had visions of a mini bayonet charge with myself as the dummy. The officer came in, we saluted and he said 'Rice-ka?' I said yes and lifted the lids off one, two and four. He sniffed, said 'OK', saluted and left. He had either lost his olfactory process altogether or was in a benign mood, as no further action was taken and we had the best meal for months!

On 23 October we transferred from the Great World to River Valley Road Camp, an emergency unit constructed of planks and attap for use by the native population or troops when the balloon went up. It swarmed with ants and bugs and we now slept on planking about two feet from the ground, but the huts were cool and airy, in contrast to the stifling hall we had just left. That apart, it was a move we faced with some trepidation as rumours had been rampant for some months about a long journey north, a river crossing and then a long march. I should explain that we now knew that rumours were rife in POW camps, some initiated because Satan finds some mischief still for idle minds to do, and some with the idea of raising the spirits of the inhabitants – 'rations have been increased'; 'peace talks have commenced in Europe'; 'new camps with showers are being built' – but when these failed to mature the resulting depression was even more acute. It must be acknowledged that some of these were a 'blind' to defeat any Japanese eavesdroppers, as radios (known as dicky birds) had now been built, and the dissemination of news had to be very strictly limited; subsequent events proved that discovery resulted in beating to death – over as many agonising days as possible.

However, this rumour proved to have very solid foundations. On 5 November 1942 we were put on standby to move on 8 November but with the vacillation that we had now come to expect from our hosts, this was postponed to the following day. On the 8th we ate the last of a very meagre

48

Red Cross issue made a few days previously, and on the 9th we marched to Singapore Station carrying all our worldly possessions – in my case a mess-tin, spoon, groundsheet, blanket, Bible, silver pencil (a birthday present from Lee Choon Eng), and the diaries on which this book is based – and I was among the more richly endowed.

We were told while on the platform that we were to be treated like English gentlemen, which shows how far the concept of Occident by Orient (and vice versa!) diverges, and how the twain never will meet, for we were now literally herded into metal trucks six feet six inches high, seven feet wide and fifteen feet long, with no windows but a sliding door on each side. Each truck had thirty two men with possessions, plus food for the anticipated journey, crammed into it. It should be recorded that the Malayan Railways had more than enough coaches to carry us but that would have indicated both indulgence and weakness on the part of the Imperial Japanese Army, two failings that they never exhibited where we were concerned. We moved off at 1700 hours after the usual screamings, bowings and salutings by which the Japanese traditionally demonstrated their military competence, and immediately discovered a further cause of discomfort: rice trucks may be adequately sprung for carrying large amounts of rice, but the process becomes virtually solid metal when only thirty-two humans form the load, and the only place on which we had to sit was the metal floor. Not all thirty-two could sit simultaneously in those confines, of course, and as one or two were ill with dysentery or malaria and had to lie down our space was further diminished. For the healthy it was largely a case of standing-room only. Thanks to our inexperience, what we had not foreseen was that by day the metal walls were so hot, and by night so cold, that the sides couldn't be touched. Thus we travelled, hunched together, in a dark, noisy, smelly hell in which conversation was almost impossible. By day the doors were kept open for ventilation and for viewing the magnificent scenery, and occasionally by night, but in both episodes so that we could allow our dysentery patients to relieve themselves: we hung on to their hands and prayed that no signal posts would tear them from our grasp. Thank God that no prescience revealed to us that we should be on the train until 3 December.

For those who had eyes to see, the journey did have compensations: the Malayan peninsula is beautiful throughout its entire length, a combination of trees, flowers, water and mountains that I imagine is unsurpassed anywhere in the world and all that beauty complemented by the flashing colours of tropical birds, and sunrises and sunsets, moonrises and moonsets, on a magnificent scale.

It was one such moonrise that contributed towards one of the greater events of my life. During a pause in the journey and while a full moon was ascending I spoke to a person whom I had met only once previously – in Alexandra Barracks on that June Sunday in 1941 when Adolf Hitler stabbed his boon companion in the back and invaded Russia. John Collinson, Royal Corps of Signals, and I commenced a mutually-sustaining and life-saving friendship that lives as brightly today as at any time in the past. I gratefully record my indebtedness to him, for reasons that I hope will become apparent in this narrative.

Our journey took us through Kuala Lumpur and Prai and on 12 November we crossed the border into Siam (Thailand); and there, as the commencement of one of the war's greatest disasters, our troubles began.

At 1130 hours our train jumped the rails and proceeded on a highly erratic course along sleepers and ballast until it was brought to an upright halt, too near to the edge of the embankment for anyone's happiness. It was restored to the track by a party of POW coolies but the prospect was far from comforting. We had now left the mountains of northern Malaya and were on the rice-growing flatland of Southern Siam, an area stretching beyond the horizon. But this was the end of the monsoon season, and I read after the war that the floods were the worst for forty years. Everywhere was desolation, the bloated bodies of humans and animals, houses and vehicles, huts and trees floating by; and, on areas of higher ground, animals bellowing in fear of their imminent death.

After several miles with our train wheels under water we stopped at Chumphong station as the line and embankment were reported to be washed away immediately ahead. The totally inadequate stocks of food issued for the journey were now part of history, and as we were marooned it appeared unlikely that more would be forthcoming. Perhaps the proximity of the village allowed the Imperial Japanese Army to commandeer provisions as we were now given four level dessertspoons of rice twice per day and a spoonful of very watery waterbuffalo stew on each occasion. The pangs of hunger now returned with a vengeance, and the occupancy of an adjacent tree by three vultures for several days did nothing to reassure us. When the water-buffalo stew ended we were issued with four small blades of grass as an alternative, and this was cut each day from a local garden. As in all such floods, the area abounded in snakes of many varieties but we were insufficiently oriental-ised to recognise their food value: that came on a much later occasion.

So far as the local population were concerned we were something of a peep-show and they gathered on the station platform each day to watch us eat, work and bathe in the waters of the flooded football pitch. Our officer in charge, whom I had known in the more salad days of peace-time Singapore, was something of a Blimp and decided to augment our tree-felling and log-splitting with PT. In view of our hunger and the total inability to apply King's Regulations it says something for our discipline that he wasn't brought to an untimely end. The very obvious effects of all this physical effort on a grossly under-nourished and sick personnel eventually penetrated even his IQ and we resumed a more normal pace.

On 22 November the water had fallen sufficiently to allow the train to continue, and we travelled until midnight when we dossed down on the grass at the edge of the line for four hours. We travelled for a further two hours and when we finally halted it was more than apparent that no further rail travel need be contemplated at the moment: the wheels were again partly submerged. Rumour had it that the Indian driver was repeatedly beaten up but he refused to obey the Japanese because his 'sixth sense' told him that there were grave dangers ahead. This perception proved to be more than justified when, after a march of four miles, carrying our kit and cooking utensils, we found the rails, most of whose sleepers had been torn away, suspended over turbulent water through which poured all the detritus of the up-country destruction. At that point the embankment had been twenty five to thirty feet high, and gaps varied in length: long enough at least to have swallowed our entire train.

For some reason which is best known only to the oriental mind it was decided that the filling of these gaps should be undertaken during the hours of darkness, and at least we had the advantage of the full moon which we had so greatly admired a day or two previously. Our base was the village of Bankwai: and as there was no accommodation available we built stick and groundsheet tents on the higher ground, more to keep out the worst invasion of flies and mosquitoes that we had met than to protect us from the weather. The flies filled our ears, eyes and noses in maddening swarms, totally defeated sleep and made work in the dark hours almost impossible. It was bad enough to work through the whole night in knee-deep mud and carrying baskets of the wretched stuff on our heads and dripping all over our bodies without having plagues of these tiny creatures to drive us to the edge of insanity.

But life has its compensations if you know how to find them, and two now presented themselves to me. Although we had now signed forms to acknowledge that we would be shot if we were caught fraternising or trading with the natives we continued to do so. They would buy watches, rings, pens, pencils, lighters, clothes – anything that was of value to them: and they got many bargains as well as many duds. After almost ten months of highly-frugal captivity stocks were very low, and I was determined to keep the watch and ring given to me by my fiancée and the silver pencil and cigarette case given to me by Lee Choon Eng.

John Collinson had a few tikals left and bought a hand of bananas and six eggs, all of which he insisted I share with him. Of course, one has to be really hungry to realise just how generous this is on behalf of the donor and how tempting it is for the would-be beneficiary to accept. I accepted.

During the hours of darkness I was aware of a northern

voice that entertained those around him with stories of those people whom he had encountered on his insurance round. When opportunity presented itself I sought him out, and he, John Collinson and I perfected that friendship throughout the many vicissitudes of our entire captivity and remain in frequent contact to this day.

Eventually the slipping and slithering and jumping five foot gaps between the sleepers and being soaked all day and finding snakes in one's blanket at night came to an end. We levelled the track, added the ballast, the rails, the fishplates and the nuts and bolts and entrained for pastures new. On 3 December 1942, at 0300 hours, we detrained at Ban Pong; and what had seemed a portion of hell became, with hindsight, an episode of idle indulgence! In twenty-five days we had covered approximately 1,000 miles in conditions of extreme discomfort, hunger, tropical disease and danger. To those were now to be added physical violence, starvation and death on a truly cataclysmic scale.

For the uninitiated, and for those of post-war generations who have no recollection of that war, it may be sensible to add a few explanations.

What happens to captives is very much a matter of the outlook of their captors – as individuals as well as the outlook of their governments. Germany, as a signatory of the Geneva Convention, respected, by and large, the rights of their military captives: they were allowed post from home, Red Cross allocations of food, cigarettes and medical equipment, were housed and clothed, provided with medical services, and at least belonged to the same ethnic group as their captors, with, basically, a common religion. Indeed, many POWs from the European and Middle East theatres have admitted that their greatest enemy was boredom. Of course there were brutalities: thugs like Hitler and Goering breed such atrocities, and there are always those down the chain of command who are happy to seek the pursuit of greater glory and authority for themselves. However, apart from forced marches and the assassination of escaping prisoners most of the violence emanating from Germany was directed at civilians, particularly Jews, and one is still incredulous that any so-called human mind could plan and execute the extermination of ten million people, after

53

brutally robbing, starving, and transporting them to the gas chambers or to execution pits.

As I have already said, the Japanese justified their evil by claiming that they no longer upheld the Geneva Convention, and were not bound by any humanitarian code. Furthermore, they suffered an acute *embarras de richesse* so far as the number of captives was concerned, as I feel that even their wildest expectations never anticipated the total collapse of British, Dutch, and American defences in South East Asia in so short a time. Accommodating, messing, neutralising and clothing such a vast number was quite beyond either their ability or their intention; and despite the huge resources of medical equipment and hospitals in the over-run countries the Imperial Japanese Army had no intention of allowing either military or civilian personnel to benefit, and shipped to Japan everything that could be transported.

All Japan's apologists, particularly those seeking investment in this country or trade contact with Tokyo, have used the excuse that Japan had a harsh code of military discipline for its own troops. No one would deny that, and numerous examples may be quoted from those years.

But it was as devoted followers of the Marquis de Sade that they merited the greatest criticism, and this was true of their treatment of birds and animals as well as of humans, and surely this could hardly be justified on grounds of discipline. Torture, pain, suffering, violence and agony would bring them to an ecstasy of pleasure both individually and collectively, and where no suitable example was available they would snatch a totally innocent bystander, and their rapt satisfaction was proportionate to their victim's agony, and was expressed in bursts of laughter and weeping satisfaction. These were no isolated incidents: they were observed from Nanking to Manchuria and throughout the whole of South East Asia, against all the creatures of the community and from the lowest private to the most senior commander, and included cannibalism. Little wonder that Nakasone and Takeshita *et al.* are seeking to re-write Japanese history!

54

Nothing in our experience had prepared us for Ban Pong. The attap roofs were more conspicuous for their holes than for their fronds, and thanks to the enormous monsoon of 1942 the latrines continued to overflow, both through the huts and along the 'paths'. The entire camp was infested with large rats which fed on everything that presented itself. The beds were continuous planking, which assured the highest tenancy of bed-bugs in the interstices. Thanks to the accumulation of static water in the surrounding area mosquitoes and other insects swarmed in their millions, our clothes and blankets were perpetually wet, and the stench of death and decomposition was ever-present. No wonder that to malaria and dysentery we now added diphtheria. The only deficit was in our manure rice, with its rat-dung, weevils and maggots – and hunger and beriberi reached new proportions. The Japanese issued a blindingly obvious recommendation that all water should be boiled – but failed to provide even the humble petrol-tins or the means to make fires towards this desirable end.

The only light that shone in that dolorous episode in Ban Pong was provided by the Roman Catholic priests and nuns from the adjacent mission station who provided us with food and dressings, and were an oasis of love and compassion in an area of considerable mental and physical suffering. This small narrative duly records our profound corporate gratitude, particularly on behalf of those men who never again saw home or loved ones.

However, of all the native Siamese with whom we came into direct contact one name stands out with brilliant clarity, and there can be few people who passed through Siam who were not, directly or indirectly, helped by this courageous man.

Boon Pong bore a most apt first name so far as the English language was concerned, and his many boons extended to every member of the allied forces. His pom-pom boat, laden with eggs, fruit, cigarettes, soap, and other provisions, chugged up the river at frequent intervals, and all POWs were the beneficiaries: his prices were the lowest

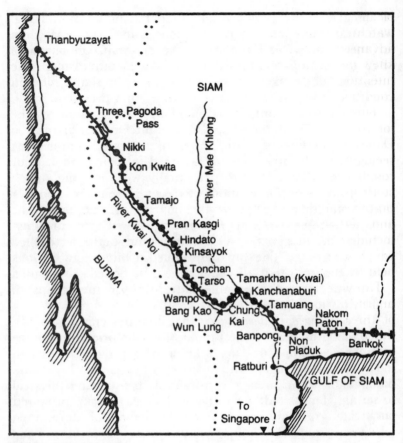

BURMA SIAM RAILWAY

56

of any trader, he accepted goods-in-lieu (many of which – watches, pens, and the like – were useless) and even advanced sums of a hundred tikals against IOUs which he knew were unlikely to be honoured, however good the intentions of the recipients, bearing in mind the prevailing conditions.

This happy and generous gentleman was a natural prey for the avaricious, brutal Japs. They demanded their Danegeld for allowing him to trade and, on the pretext of seeing him as a spy, damaged his goods with bayonet and rough handling. They beat him up with harsh regularity, stole from him unblushingly and created every possible problem for him both in loading and off-loading his craft; and all this was particularly true when his manifest included drugs which he had discovered at base and for which we had provided the capital from very meagre funds held by the medical staff.

He was a hero in every sense of the word because, unarmed, he faced a brutal and malign foe, and at the end of three-and-a-half years of every indignity and brutality that could be inflicted his courage and cheerfulness were undimmed.

He totally deserved the decoration awarded by Buckingham Palace in the post-war years; indeed, it would be true to say that many courageous men on the allied side received far higher decorations for considerably less valour.

How true it is that great endeavours frequently have small beginnings. On 7 December a small detachment was taken out from Ban Pong in the charge of an insignificant Imperial Japanese Army private, and in a small fenced cul-de-sac we were ordered to begin laying sleepers which were already stacked nearby. To these we added lines and fish plates, and the lines were spiked to the sleepers by hammers. Only then was the ballast added, a typical Japanese back-to-front process which was to be repeated in 1943. The work was extremely heavy as each rail had to be lifted and carried in pincers, and we worked from 0900 to 2000 hours daily. To the surprise of both ourselves and the

Japanese we laid eleven kilometres in twelve days, but this was easily beaten as we became more proficient.

Thus commenced what was to become one of the major tragedies of the war, the Railway of Death, as it is now commonly known. Some very foolish statistics have been given in relation to it: shortly after the war 250,000 dead was given in a national newspaper, but it is now reasonably reduced to 150,000 by most authorities. This covers all service personnel and the many Asiatics who were so cruelly impressed by the Japanese in Malaya and Singapore but it does not include all those throughout the world who have died since, nor the many thousands of mental and physical cripples, the blind and the deaf.

In the beginning the Burma/Siam railway wasn't a Japanese concept. Before the end of the last century the entire area had been surveyed with the idea of joining the two countries from Bangkok to Rangoon, thus avoiding the long haul by sea around Singapore for ships from China and Hong Kong en route to Rangoon. Similarly, Britain and the USA had more than one survey before the Second World War. It is reported that all had been abandoned on humanitarian grounds, despite enormous strides in mechanized rail-laying and advances in the field of tropical hygiene and medicine. Mountain ranges, fast-flowing rivers, annual monsoons of six-months' duration, recurring epidemics of malaria, bacillary and amoebic dysentery, cholera and the ever-prevalent hookworm defeated any such project at the outset and the scheme was finally abandoned in the thirties.

However, the Japanese Government was never to suffer such inhibitions, particularly on humanitarian grounds, in the building of the railway, the Mergui Road, or any of the other major projects that caused such an appalling loss of life throughout South East Asia. There was an apparently inexhaustible supply of what the Japanese were pleased to call their 'white coolies' and 'white elephants', and what better use to put them to than a major war effort that would transport their troops and war material on a direct north/south route from Singapore via Bangkok to Moulmein and Rangoon by rail, and thence by land and sea to the conquest of India? It eliminated the use of troopships and naval escorts on the Japanese side, and the risk of encounter with the British and US Forces operating from India and Colombo.

And so, without even a glimmer of what lay ahead, we soldiered on. The food showed no signs of improvement, despite the heavy work and longer hours. We now began to have that appalling concoction, boiled pumpkin, to add to the rice. It tasted so awful that we decided to give the excess to a pig farmer who worked nearby. He stuck his fingers in the contents and then in his mouth, and said, 'No good, no good, pigs all die' – and gave the tin back to us.

I never really got to the bottom of the Siamese currency, and I know of no one else who did, but my diary at that time records that one tikal = 100 staar. The Japanese were supposed to pay us at regular intervals but this was conspicuous more in the breach than in the observance. We could buy one duck or hen egg for 5 staar; small bananas fifteen for 10 staar; pommeloes ten staar each; Virginian cigarettes ten for 15 staar but they were of very poor quality. Such things were always obtained under threat of dire punishment if the Japanese or Korean guards should invoke the law relating to trading with natives, as they often did. In theory we were paid if we worked, but this was only in such small amounts that several days' pay was required in order to buy one or two eggs or bananas; and it was a moral obligation to share one's income with those who were sick or undergoing prolonged convalescence as when recovering from dysentery or beriberi. It was our experience througout captivity that the Japanese are natural liars; and would promise camps with showers and lights, extra food, drugs, and so on, and these were never forthcoming. As we had no financial checks it was a matter of simple logic to conclude that they were equally dishonest with pay and food; and we came across numerous instances in confirmation.

On 23 December we worked until 1500 hours, returned to Ban Pong, and finally said goodbye to that focus of all filth in our move to Non Pladuk, three miles south, and now railhead for our construction efforts. The last of the monsoon water had now gone – to be replaced by dried mud, and all movement on foot involved suffocating dust which penetrated lungs, eyes and ears and reduced visibility to about twenty feet. As Non Pladuk was an increasing Japanese base there was a fairly constant flow of traffic but the water supply was by borehole and totally inadequate so we were never able to remove the dust, either from ourselves or from our clothes. So as we had no soap and no water we reverted to type and grew beards, moustaches and long hair – all further irritants in that intense tropical heat,

BURMA-SIAM RAILWAY PROJECT 1942/43.
BUILT BY ALLIED PRISONERS OF WAR

1. Diesel lorry – usually pushing 8–10 'Trucks'
2. Pivots for delivering rails to track
3. Sleepers
4. Bag of fishplates, nuts and bolts
5. Horn-operated signal lights

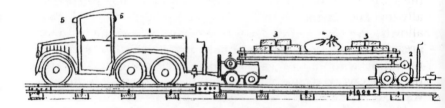

Drawn from memory after almost 45 years
(and certainly not to scale)

and made worse by the total absence of salt in our diet and the ensuing skin eruptions.

The supply, construction and maintenance of the railway involved so many Heath Robinson contraptions and improvisations that it is still a miracle to many of us that it ever achieved completion. The only source of power during construction was the road/rail diesel lorry, which was simply driven above the rails, the road-wheels were removed and it was lowered on to the rails, now using its metal wheels. They were enormously powerful vehicles and were obviously built for the sole purpose of towing several tons of bogies, lines, sleepers and fishplates.

Their great disadvantage was that being basically a road

vehicle, they spent fifty per cent of their time being driven backwards – often over distances of many miles. As their drivers were, theoretically, at least human, they soon cricked their necks, and turned to face the direction from which they had come! This, plus the fact that, on many occasions, they couldn't see past a load of standing prisoners, caused many accidents, particularly during the hours of darkness.

Each bogie consisted of four wheels with a small platform at one end, through which ran a brake control to the two nearer wheels. There was a further platform squarely above the wheels, and at the diagonal centre of this was a sturdy metal pin about six inches high and two inches in diameter. This pin held the master rail when two bogies were joined and the other rails were laid in parallel alongside it. The sleepers were mounted transversely on the rails and the nuts and bolts and fishplates carried on the excess areas of the two platforms. A pair of wheels was mounted horizontally on the upper, outer edge of each platform and this allowed the rails to be shot forward on to the sleepers. The great snag was that the bogies had to be manhandled off the rails when empty, and on again when returning to base, as the gadget to facilitate this was never there when it was wanted.

If a waggon was needed the base was already provided with a central hole at each end, and these fitted over the pins on the bogies; upright ends and sides could be added to complete the container.

The flat base was the one most often used to transport personnel up and down the line and catastrophic injuries often resulted. The track at this time was so badly ballasted that the people sitting round the edge were the sole support of those standing, and violent lateral movement always threatened to throw everyone on to the side of the track. If the sitters didn't tuck their heels firmly into the H girder running right around the platform there was always a possibility of dangling legs striking signal posts and of feet being amputated by platforms – and I know of two cases where men had their feet mutilated in this way.

On Christmas Eve 1942 I became a victim of this. A rather gormless Royal Northumberland Fusilier allowed his legs to dangle and when the anticipated signal post was reached he drew his legs up so sharply that he knocked mine off the girder and they struck the post. By great good fortune I was wearing a pair of South African field boots, with stout heel plates, issued to me only a day or two previously. I assume that my left heel struck a wheel flange as the plate and heel were subsequently found to be cut to a depth of half-an-inch. As the train was doing approximately thirty mph, I did a wonderful parabola on to the adjoining rails of the Singapore/Bangkok line, landing with the middle of my back on the rail. Despite John Collinson's protests the train continued its journey – the Japanese private assuring John that I was dead.

My left knee, right hip, shoulder and back were all now bleeding fairly briskly, and the rail had severely bruised my back; but my ankles presented the greatest problem: both were swelling rapidly and I felt the left was broken. I was able to signal to a lorry approaching on a side road and its two Australian occupants very kindly came over, cut off my boots and carried me to their vehicle and thence to Non Pladuk. As the huts were then under construction we had no bamboo beds. As I passed through a partly-built hut a Japanese soldier severely beat me with a plank, despite the fact that my ankles now appeared to be the victims of elephantiasis. I lay for the remainder of the day on the mud but when the final bugle blew I inched my way to the latrine – only to be punched violently in the face for a thrown-down cigarette end which certainly didn't come from me, but the Jap soldier didn't bother to confirm that. I went to bed with the firm conviction that it hadn't been my day.

So far as the Japanese intentions to make war were concerned, the lorries, bogies, fish-plates and other rail material told an eloquent tale. While the lorries could certainly be used on the road, their primary use was obviously intended to be on the construction of the railway: their wheels were flanged so that they could be lowered onto rails as soon as the outer tyred wheels had been removed, and their engine power was far too great for any potential load on the vehicle itself. They were fitted with couplings and buffers, and the braking lights near the roof of each cab were obviously there for signalling for the following bogie brakes to be applied in emergencies.

Bearing in mind the many hundreds of bogies required, and the platforms, ends and sides to convert the bogies into waggons, it is apparent that the planning and construction of such an enterprise required far more time than the period between the commencement of the war in December 1941 and the commencement of the line-laying in December 1942.

All this had been planned on a long-term basis, as had the removal of bridges in other parts of South East Asia so that the 'River Kwai' bridge, at least, could be built on time.

On Christmas Day we had the following banquet, in great contrast to the food of the previous ten months:

Breakfast: Boiled rice (with the usual debris), fish rissole and sweet milkless coffee

Lunch: Boiled rice, scrambled eggs, meat and vegetable stew, sweet milkless coffee

Dinner: Boiled rice, battered steak, meat and vegetable stew, doughnut, sweet milkless tea

(The rissoles and doughnuts were made with rice-flour, and I think the tinned meat and vegetable stew may have been left by the British).

We had a concert that evening devised by our POWs and rather prejudiced a possible repeat by demanding 'The King' at the end. Two thousand lusty voices took it up spontaneously, despite the screamed obscenities of our Japanese audience. The louder they yelled the louder we sang. Rifle butts, feet and fists were generously used by the Imperial Japanese Army, but we sang it through fortissimo to the last word. Wonderful.

We resumed work on the following day and now learnt that our stint was to be 1200 yards per day. In order to achieve this the Japanese resorted to a new tactic which was to be increasingly used as the line advanced: they forced the 'light' sick who should have been inside in camp to work on the line, and the bedfast to get up and take their place on camp duties. Protests by camp commandants and medical officers were of no avail, and usually resulted in the protesters being severely beaten. It was always stated that the Japanese referred to us as animals, and they were obviously prepared to treat us as such; indeed one Japanese officer, on being offered elephants to haul trees from the jungle for bridge-building, is reported to have replied that he already had his elephants – white elephants.

As my ankle was now confirmed as broken and my knee wound had turned septic I was allowed to remain in the camp – on condition that I undertook the duties of both messing NCO and orderly corporal, both of which involved considerable walking and standing. However, I was in much better condition than many as beriberi, malaria and dysentery continued to play havoc throughout the camps because of prolonged starvation, intensive labour and the increasing brutality of our captors, both Japanese and Korean.

On 23 January 1943 we moved several miles north 'to a camp adjacent to rail-head named Tahrua and it now seemed that we were to be the permanent rail-laying party. To a certain extent we became the victims of our own efficiency, as the Japanese increased the daily stint to the allocated time. We worked very much as a team, and only changed our work-pattern to accommodate the sick and absent. However, with what we regarded as another example of Japanese inefficiency, we were creating a problem as we advanced that was to cost us dear in the coming months: we were laying the sleepers directly on to the mud trace of the line without ballast, and while this allowed the line to forge ahead at a tremendous rate it meant that, come laden trains and the intensity of the monsoon rains, the line would be deadly dangerous and probably useless. What we didn't know at that time was that the Japanese engineers had promised Tokyo that the line would be through to Rangoon by mid-August of that year. The attempt to justify that promise was to cause much mental and physical suffering, many accidents, and thousands of lives.

The earliest parties had moved from Singapore to Siam in June of 1942 – whence came the original rumours of the long journey – and these people had been clearing the jungle, building embankments, blasting and digging the cuttings, and building bridges and culverts. Bearing in mind the density of the jungle, the enormous height of the trees, and the primitive nature of the tools and equipment it was little wonder that the incidence of disease and accidents had reached truly horrific dimensions. It was along this route that we laid sleepers, dropped the rails, fastened the fish-plates and spiked the rails; all in equatorial heat, on rice that was cooked on the previous night and carried in our mess-tins, and with a totally inadequate water supply for drinking.

On 30 January we moved from Tahrua to Kanchanaburi, to huts whose attap roofs were collapsing, bamboo beds were riddled with bugs, bamboo supports were swarming with a new phenomenon – bamboo lice – and where each man was allocated fourteen inches of bed-space for both self and kit. As usual, latrines were totally inadequate for the numbers involved and swarmed with dysentery fly. However, as 3 February was my birthday we decided to celebrate and John Collinson and I shared six scrambled eggs, one kilo of boiled sweet potatoes, biscuits, coffee – and bananas 'borrowed' from an adjacent plantation. I noted at the time that the total cost of this hedonistic indulgence was 6½d. in English equivalent: at least we had something to talk about for several days.

From 1 February the pay for NCOs and ORs rose from 10 staar to 25 staar per day on account of the 'heavy nature of our work' – i.e. from 1.45d. per day to just over 3d. (at 240 pence to the £). This, of course, was real filthy lucre – wealth beyond the dreams of avarice – and paid only for the days on which one worked – no work, no pay.

On 18 February my heel was examined by a senior British MO, who confirmed that the fracture had healed with the nerve trapped. On the following day the heel was injected with Novocaine, my boot was forced on and I returned to work on the line.

This now involved crossing what has become known through books, films, radio/TV as the *Bridge Over the River Kwai*. The film, while excellent entertainment, insulted the memory of every person who had worked on that infamous project. We did not go out to work dressed in full khaki drill with bush hats, long hose, boots, and wearing watches and rings, and whistling Colonel Bogey. We went as coolies, with

Tamarkhan Bridge, Siam.
(erroneously known as the Kwai Bridge)

only our pride and the grandeur of the human spirit to support us – a point on which the Siamese and even the Japanese congratulated us on many occasions.

There were actually two bridges over the River Mae Khlong north of Kanchanaburi – a wooden one, which was built to allow the railway to go through, and the much longer concrete and metal one whose construction took so high a toll in health and lives. From the first coffer dams, with their thousands of tons of filling and cement, to the finished spans, it was built by POW labour, and remains to this day a symbolic epitaph to all who laboured on it.

The wooden bridge was one of the first projects undertaken by POW labour, as the Imperial Japanese Army realised that the Mae Khlong was a major barrier to most of the work further north. Certainly the jungle with its massive hardwood trees could be cleared, huts could be built, and buildings, cuttings and trace brought into operation but the essential features of sleepers and rails would halt at the river's edge. So enormous hardwood stakes, sharpened at one end, were floated out into mid-stream, held upright by POWs and driven into the river-bed by primitive pile-drivers whose ropes were operated manually for hour after monotonous hour by further gangs of prisoners. The pyramids were probably built in the same way by brutal and sadistic overseers, careless of the cost in lives and health to their slaves and with the same monotonous chanting to ensure a strict tempo and equality of effort. It is still possible to recall the 'Ichi-nee-ne-say-oo, ne-sayoo' that accompanied every lift of the weight to the apex of the pile-driver – and the resulting torn and bleeding hands at the end of each day.

So many things were now militating against survival that eventual completion of the line can only be seen as a testimony to the will to survive, and to the subjugation of the ills of the body by the spirit of self-preservation. The combination of a temperature of 110°, lack of water, manure rice, the continuous incidence of beriberi, dysentery and malaria, a shattering work-load and the increasing brutality of our Japanese and Korean guards made the will to sustain life weaken at times; and many men simply lay down, gave up the struggle and died. This hadn't the slightest effect on

68

the Imperial Japanese Army who simply called on their vast reserves in South East Asia for replacements.

The Koreans, who had been subordinate to Tokyo for many years, were treated with arrogant contempt and violence by the Japanese, who were totally hated in return. The upshot was that when they fell out we became the victims – of rifle butts, boots, teak-sticks, rocks, lumps of earth and so forth. The Koreans were never allowed rank of any sort, but their right to ill-treat us was never questioned, and thus we bore the brunt of their spleen. Self-defence by us was never permitted as this was seen as defiance of the entire Japanese system and was treated in highly summary fashion – usually by death.

One of the most conspicuous lacks throughout captivity was of basic communication. In a similar situation in Europe we could probably have got by without too many difficulties but the finer technical points of both line-laying and bridge-building were usually outlined in soil or sand with a stick, and woe to them who failed to comprehend. Most of the Japanese and Koreans appeared to be rice coolies, fishermen and labourers who were unable either to read or to calculate, and this was admitted by a Japanese officer in the early days who, when asked to give us access to the many thousands of books in Singapore, replied that he didn't believe that all British personnel could read as his soldiers certainly couldn't.

The assumption that no Japanese could speak English was a dangerous one, and led to complications on more than one occasion, as any outspoken comment was unlikely to be favourable to that nation.

During the line construction two Japanese privates attempted to tell John Collinson and me how they wanted a siding built from main line to the riverside. After drawing many diagrams with sticks on the sandy river-edge we failed to understand the finer points of their project and in desperation I said to John, 'I wish these little b......s could speak English.'

This provoked howls of laughter from one of the Japanese who then said to his companion, 'He wishes we little b......s could speak English.' He was, of course, correct both in grammar and syntax, but both of them could have saved us a great deal of time if their original orders had been given in our language. As least they took the comment in good part and we learnt a lesson that lasted throughout the remainder of captivity.

One of the greatest rewards in this polyglot community in which we lived was the kindness and generosity of the Thais, just as it had been with the Chinese and Malayans in Singapore. Whatever had been the reactions of these natives in both countries when the Japanese arrived, they now hated the Japanese with a fervour equal to our own. In Singapore we had been embarrassed by the generosity shown us by the impoverished people, all of whom told us that they longed for the return of the British; coffee, cold drinks and food were served to us at great risk to the donors, purses or wads of notes were thrown from balconies, and cigarettes and cheroots were given to us by passing individuals. Until we had left the native areas behind and were deep in the jungle we received the same kindness from the Thais, who gave us bananas, eggs, peanut toffee, tapioca-flour biscuits – and asked nothing in return.

On 12 March we moved to Ban Kaow, twenty-five miles north of Kanchanaburi, and thus our daily crossing of the Mae Khlong came to an end but the new camp was sited on the edge of the River Kwai Noi and thus we were able to bathe daily on our return from the line. We had no soap, of course, and towels were a superfluous luxury in such heat, but the sybaritic pleasure of nipping one's nostrils and totally submerging was beyond description, and was usually followed by taking handfuls of sand from the river-bed and scraping away the dirt and sweat. However, the contra-indications of such pleasure were almost imme-diately apparent as we received messages from up-country that cholera had broken out – and cholera is a virulent waterborne disease.

If we retained our sanity and sustained our bodies throughout these tribulations it was due in large measure to the friendships we formed and the inter-dependence we all recognised. We worked from first light (breakfast of boiled rice was usually eaten in darkness), until 18–2000 hours, and thereafter we sat in darkness until what was euphemistically called 'lights out'. One or two of the more optimistic spirits would buy pig-oil, in which they inserted string and lit the latter, but this guttering tribute to Lucifer was useless for reading and was too-easily spilt: so we sat in darkness and imagined the greater light. How we longed for books and letters from home, and hot baths and toothpaste, razor blades and soap – civilisation!

While on the indelicate subject of toilet paper: my diary records that in early 1943 we were issued with twenty-five sheets – so far as I remember the only issue made throughout captivity. Considering the state of our diet and bodily functions this was used on the day that it was received. This typifies the thinking of the Japanese; we were crying out for drugs, dressings, surgical instruments etc., of which they had an abundance but they chose to issue twenty-five sheets of poor-quality toilet paper to thousands of POWs. Throughout our days in Siam we used leaves from the surrounding trees but there were dangers and problems here as well: many of the leaves carried thousands of minute needles on the underside and these caused the most intense irritation, and in static camps so great was the demand that forays of ever-increasing depths had to be made into the jungle, thus providing the Japanese with the excuse to beat up the offenders; where there was a bamboo perimeter fence insuperable problems were encountered when the trees had been stripped.

To return to the subject of friendship: one doubts if there is a FEPOW anywhere in the world who wouldn't attribute his survival to the dedication of his friends, and stories underlining this are legion. Trips at night-time 'through the bamboo' to buy Emetine, quinine and food for sick companions (punishable by death on return), the nursing of those with dysentery, cholera and diphtheria which often resulted in the nurse becoming the victim and losing his life, the sharing of pay with a sick and therefore payless friend, the surrender of a blanket to sustain a companion: volumes could be written on this subject alone.

It has been repeatedly remarked that such camaraderie appeared to be entirely absent in the Japanese forces, both in the flush of victory and in approaching defeat. It may be that they saw giving and receiving of comradely help as an admission of weakness and therefore of loss of face, but I never recall, on even one occasion, a Japanese giving a drink of water, a cigarette or a helping hand to a deserving comrade, and this was never more apparent than in the final days of the Greater East Asia Co-prosperity Sphere when retreating Japanese troops, many of them wounded, sick and starving, were treated with contempt by the camp guards. It is to the enormous credit of the British troops that, in that period, after years of violence, neglect and genocide, it was they who took water, their few treasured cigarettes, and scarce food and gave them to the suffering Japanese, some of whom, remembering the earlier years, wept with gratitude.

So, while friendship, as we know it, was totally absent among the Japanese, it became our very life-blood, and we sustained each other morally, mentally and physically. When the snake-pits and the Black Dogs of depression were apparent there was always someone to give words of encouragement, to point to the years ahead, to loved ones, and to the promise of a brighter future. Beriberi is always accompanied by loss of memory and concentration, and we stimulated each other's mental processes by recalling families, holidays, books, and in planning the future; and we drove each other, and eavesdroppers, mad by talking about food – menus, past and to come, and the succulence of roast beef and pork, the delectableness of fruit cake, and what we would give for a simple bag of fish and chips in newspaper. Remember that our water was chlorinated or boiled, our rice spiced with manure, maggots and weevils, and without the benefit of salt, pepper or sugar.

Throughout the greater part of the railway construction I had the unstinting friendship of four people: John Collinson, Stan Henson, Les Harrison and Cyril Huckerby. Poor Huckerby died shortly after his release, as a result of those privations, but the others are still alive and we are all in frequent contact. No man could have wished for better stalwarts through such dire events, and I shall be for ever in their debt for their generosity in both the spiritual and material things of life.

One of the great advantages of being on the line-laying party was that our supply-base was always behind us, and we always had transport from and to camp. This also meant that our rice could frequently be brought to us freshly cooked, instead of being cooked on the previous night and being carried in rusty mess-tins until eaten. On the rare occasions when there was meat on the menu, this was kept for the evening meal, as any attempt to transport it during the day resulted in the arrival of stinking rubbish which had to be thrown away. Pumpkin stew could be transported but it was revolting even by starvation standards and probably had no dietary value. At least it was a change of flavour.

The very conditions whose recognition had prompted the abandonment of earlier plans to build a line to Moulmein/Rangoon were now obvious so far as all those thousands of troops to the north of us were concerned. Because we were working through virgin jungle there were no roads to the up-country camps, and as the water of the Kwae Noi dropped so the shallow-draught supply boats known as pom-poms were unable to go to the camps, even where these were adjacent to the river; where they were away from the river there was no lateral communication, either by land or tributaries. There were reports that armed Japanese and POWs were going into the jungle to shoot wild animals but we never heard whether these were successful. Subsequent up-country experience suggested that there was little to shoot in that density of jungle.

The harshest and most lethal labours were undertaken by those who felled the trees, built the enormous embankments, blasted the cuttings from solid rock, adzed the green timber pulled down from the jungle, and built the many bridges. As has already been said, the people involved in these mentally and physically destructive labours had no supply base from which to draw rations, as we had with the line behind us. They relied on the river exclusively, and this posed problems in times of flood or drought.

As with all railways built in mountainous country, trace and bridge and cutting repeated their monotonous pattern from the moment we reached the Mae Khlong until the completion of the line. The ground was either impenetrable because of the heat of the sun, or was a sea of mud because of the amount of water during the six months of the

73

monsoon: either way it made the task almost impossible –particularly with such a high degree of tropical disease, hunger, accidents and the non-stop brutality of the Japanese.

If we had had adequate tools the work would have been much easier but the Japanese appeared to have little understanding of the concept. Mechanisation didn't exist, and the axes, saws, changkols and shovels were usually of such poor quality that they were a major waste both of time and effort. But failure was always blamed on the workers, not the tools. Tree and hand axes, saws and adzes were blunt and without the means for sharpening, shovels were usually without a transverse handle and had the broom variety of handle, and when the Japanese required more shovels for the speedo these were made of corrugated sheeting in their own workshops. The thin metal simply folded over when thrust into gravel or mud and even the most brutal Japanese soldier had to admit that they were useless.

Work parties clearing the jungle and preparing the bridge foundations and superstructure were usually working far ahead of the trace construction, with the intention of ensuring an uninterrupted operation. As Siam's more northern areas consist wholly of tropical rainforest the problems were formidable. Most of the trees were two-hundred feet tall with four enormous buttress roots and their upper reaches entangled with each other and densely-laced with liana – the sturdy creeper that allows Tarzan to swing so smoothly through the upper reaches of the jungle. The result was that when, after laborious hours of work, the base was sawn through, the crown refused to be parted from its siblings. The clumps of giant bamboo proved just as uncooperative, and could be cut down only one at a time and frequently showered the workers with an intensely irritating type of needle which stuck to damp bodies and could only be removed with copious water, which was rarely available and, if available, forbidden.

But even here, Mother Nature offered some apology and compensation for her more difficult children: after some months, bushes grew along the edge of the track, and night-time brought a fairy-like display of millions of fireflies twinkling on each bush. Where the track ran straight, the

74

miles of bushes put on a chain of lights that far outstripped the efforts of Blackpool in their natural beauty, and fascinated even the most exhausted of their viewers.

So the progress of the railway provided a life-line for each up-country camp that we reached, as well as for ourselves. But the process was an exhausting one both mentally and physically. A combination of a totally-inadequate diet, tropical heat, sweated labour, lack of medical facilities, persistent diarrhoea, and the psychological burdens of captivity – the lack of correspondence and news from home, and the prospect of never-ending-war – allied with an ever-increasing death rate in all camps made many people quietly give up and die. According to several of the doctors their patients suffered from many conditions but it was often the mental surrender rather than the physical illnesses that ended their lives. To cap it all, the few items of drugs and medical equipment that we had were stolen by the Siamese on 30 March 1943 and the hope of replacement was futile. We had bought all these items out of our meagre pay – mostly M & B, Emetine and quinine – and this village had no resources. Simultaneously, several of our fellows were attacked by Thais at night when moving between huts and latrines. The attackers were ugly customers and all were armed with hunting knives, against which we had no defence. They were reported to be after clothes, but a daylight examination of these would have proved the folly of their efforts as we were all now reduced to wearing rags.

However, we were far from reaching the nadir of our misfortunes, and two processes started now which were dramatically to increase our sickness and death rates and lower even further our already impoverished living conditions. On 30 March we had the first of the pre-monsoon rains and as all the huts were leaking the rice bags and blankets that we used for bedding were soon sodden. The torrential rain lasted for three days – embankments and cuttings were washed away, the camp was ankle-deep in mud, and the problems associated with laying sleepers and rails, and fastening them with fishplates and spikes proved very much greater. The Japanese hated the rain as much as we did and lashed out with butts, boots, fists and teak-sticks without provocation.

75

The second process was what subsequently became known as the 'Great Speedo'. Even the Japanese now recognised that their promise to the High Command to have the line completed to Moulmein or Rangoon by mid-August was impossible of fulfilment but in order to save as much face as possible it was necessary to go through the motions. However, as the embankment was incomplete a short way ahead, and as we had already run out of fishplates, further construction was impossible. Several of us were put on the pile-driver and for days we suffered raw hands and aching shoulders and the traditional beatings if we lost the tempo of the ropes. The attempt to manufacture fishplates was a total disaster due to failure to realise that these can only work effectively when the edges are flanged, thus ensuring that there is no 'step' as the weight of the wheels passes from one rail to the next. The Japanese simply bored four holes in a flat piece of metal of the appropriate size, and we bolted this to the rail with a piece of wood sandwiched between to act as a shock-absorber. When line-travel was recommenced we experienced four spine-shattering blows at the meeting of each pair of lines, and even the Japanese had to admit that this was a total failure. The sleepers, lines and fishplates were all certainly second-hand, the sleepers showing evidence of long use elsewhere: they were deeply indented where previous lines had passed over them, had deep bolt-holes, and frequently shattered when dropped on the ground. It was rumoured that this equipment and the spans for the 'Kwai' bridge had come from Java.

In order to invest himself with the necessary authority the Japanese soldier had a habit of what we called 'winding himself up'. This consisted of sucking air in between almost closed teeth, and the longer he went on the worse became his temper. When he had fully charged his batteries he would begin screaming maniacally, and even the few words we had learnt became lost in a torrent of inarticulate noise. I suppose this had the effect of impressing his superiors with his efficiency, particularly if he threw in a couple of beatings for good measure.

The tragedy was that such people held the power of life and death over their captives, not only in the sense of physical ill-treatment but in the making up of work-parties. The opinions and protests of our COs and MOs were of no avail and were treated as insults to the Imperial Japanese Army. Quotas had to be filled, and when those who, by stretching the imagination, had been deemed fit to work, didn't reach the required number, the acutely sick and dying were roughly handled out on to the parade. If they collapsed at work they were given lesser work – including being buried up to their armpits so that their hands were free; and if they died we buried them on the spot, said the Lord's Prayer, and continued with our work.

There were other manifestations of the Great Speedo that were equally demoralising: work was increased to two shifts per day: 0600–1700 hours, and 1700 to 0600 hours, which meant that the early shift worked for eleven hours and the second thirteen hours. On each occasion there was less than one hour allowed for the single meal of boiled rice. Traditionally we had been allowed a yasume (pronounced yassmay), of a few minutes for smoking and seeing to the needs of nature, both morning and afternoon. Most of us continued to suffer from diarrhoea because of the appalling food, but as we worked in teams it was virtually impossible to stop when nature called. The new pressure of work lessened both the rest periods, and occasionally there was none at all.

Possibly through ignorance and lack of trained staff the Japanese had never shown any inclination to maintain their rolling stock in good condition. In theory each bogie had a brake and there should have been two brakes to each load, in addition to the brakes on the six wheels of the lorry. These were by now so neglected that they were virtually useless, and many accidents resulted. Similarly the lorry had both front and rear lights, and pairs of lights at front and rear of the cab linked to the horn so that the bogie brakes could be applied in an emergency. On 18 March we had the first of many violent collisions when two trains without lights collided in the dark and one of the Dutchmen received a broken arm and severe concussion. Although I was in the first truck to be struck, I braced myself when I heard the approaching train and wasn't injured; but it was the first of many such accidents.

The first major silver lining occurred on 28 April when we had our first mail from home. I received two, written on 12 and 20 July 1942, respectively, and both were an act of faith as word hadn't been received that I was a POW. At least I knew that those at home were still alive nine months previously but they had to wait until May 1943 to learn that I was captive. Trust the Japanese to spread the agony. Subsequent mail in both directions received similar treatment, and at the end of the war many thousands of our letters were found all over South East Asia. To be fair to the Japanese, most of their so-called interpreters were totally incomprehensible in both speech and writing, and Command wasn't prepared to deliver uncensored post, I presume.

At about this time there occurred one of those rare events which remain with one for the rest of one's life. The track was now running through virgin jungle, between trees of enormous height, and there were splendid views of mountains, rivers, clouds and trees. The arrival of millions of butterflies was of such a striking nature that we all momentarily stopped work to watch, even the Japanese. It went on for several days, a continuous cylinder of fluttering movement about eight to ten feet in diameter and with wings almost touching, an enormous migratory flight of unknown origin and destination. Most of them were white or parti-coloured with white as the predominant colour. I have seen similar flights on a much smaller scale in South Africa in recent years, all very beautiful.

Of course, this brought a wonderful opportunity to kill or maim as many of the gorgeous creatures as possible, and the Japanese took full advantage of it. Their teak-sticks, acquired mainly for ill-treating their captives, could bring down a flock with a single swipe, and there they lay, their wings and bodies broken, until they died. What on earth was it that brought such pleasure to grown men that they could shout with joy at such devastation, and vie in its repetition?

The apologists for the Japanese frequently use the excuse that they were harsh with their enemies because they were harsh with each other at a military level. This, of course, is total nonsense as many thousands of people will confirm.

Even at human level their worst endeavours had nothing to do with discipline or punishment for poor effort. It was unqualified sadism. It probably satisfied their ego to beat up a six foot man when they were only five feet tall, and one can imagine the tales they told of their heroism in their nightly chats.

But neither discipline nor punishment can be used as an excuse for their ill-treatment of other creatures, in which they revelled. I was so appalled by this that in January 1943 I made a note in my diary of some of these malign obscenities – and there isn't a POW from any Far-Eastern theatre who couldn't repeat these ad nauseam.

(1) Catching wild birds of the larger variety, breaking their joints where the wings met the body, keeping them without food and water in tropical heat for two – three days, buffeting them on every possible occasion, finally tying a string to their ankles prior to whirling them overhead, and then throwing them to a puppy as a toy.

(2) Pouring fuel oil on a toad and then setting fire to it.

(3) Pushing lighted cigarettes into crabs' eyes and then letting them crawl away totally blind.

(4) Dipping a live fowl into boiling water prior to plucking.

On one occasion at Kanchanaburi a troop of Japanese soldiers threw a bitch into a pit, and proceeded to gouge and twist metal bars into every anterior and posterior hole they could find, despite its agonised screams. When they had had their fill they walked away laughing, without delivering the coup de grace. They had of course taken the wise precaution of breaking all its legs at the start so that it couldn't defend itself.

Dogs were always prime targets because, I suppose, they heightened the feeling of courage in the attacker, although most of the poor things I saw were spiritless creatures who ran away at the first sign of danger. A favourite game of the Japanese was to drive a laden lorry over a sleeping dog and then laugh with uncontrollable joy when the vultures descended to tear it to bits before a merciful death supervened.

Probably the same courage qualification applied where elephants were concerned. I have seen many Japanese, who fancied themselves as mahouts, tear holes in the heads of bellowing terrified elephants who had no idea what the madmen on their backs wanted them to do – their only instruction coming through a viciously-pointed goad. A trained mahout uses feet, voice, and gentle guidance with a stick – and the response is a miracle of communication between animal and man.

If it were true that the Japanese were as brutal to their own soldiers as to the enemy we saw little evidence of it. However, one occasion sticks in the mind and is unlikely to be eradicated.

A British soldier working on the line was attacked by a Japanese soldier for, as so often happened, no apparent reason other than boredom. He was abused so badly that, on return to camp several hours later, he was still deeply unconscious and covered in wounds that the flies were attacking voraciously.

The Japanese sergeant who came to dismiss the fatigue asked the reason for the casualty; and when this was given he asked if the FEPOWs could identify the culprit. On being assured that they could he called out the Japanese workparty and had the attacker identified. He was called to the front of the parade, knocked unconscious with one uppercut, and one eye gouged out by the sergeant's booted heel.

On being assured that the FEPOWs considered that honour was satisfied the parade was dismissed and no more was heard of the incident.

The Japanese never forwent an opportunity to inflict misery on their victims, either from the services or the civilian population. At the height of the railway speedo the edict was issued that POWs would not be allowed to visit the latrines between Lights Out and Reveille. This was totally malicious as we were in deep jungle and the possibility of escape was non-existent. The Japanese were well aware, of course, of the persistent diarrhoea afflicting almost every man in the camp and the need for several excursions to the latrine for each sufferer.

Such an imposition had three advantages to the Japanese:

(1) Retention caused maximum pain and insomnia.
(2) Incontinence fouled the huts.
(3) Any attempt to reach the latrines under cover of darkness could justify a violent beating.

There is abundant evidence, in many parts of the world, of Japanese long-term preparation for war, and of Emperor Hirohito's active involvement in it. His reign of more than sixty years covered the Panay incident, the invasion of Manchuria, the huge increase in their merchant navy in the thirties, the replacement of a largely civilian cabinet with peaceful intentions by a military cabinet with total commitment to war, and the overall strategy associated with such a step.

One is tempted to wonder, therefore, what would have happened to the Emperor if the alliance of Britain, America and Russia had been a real one instead of a paper expedient necessitated by Hitler's attack on Russia. If Hitler and Goering hadn't taken the coward's exit there is little doubt that they would have been executed after the Nuremburg trials, a similar fate would have been accorded Mussolini if his compatriots hadn't undertaken the task, and Pierre Laval paid the penalty for his supposed involvement with the collapse of France in 1940.

So it seems a parody of justice that while Terauchi, Yamashita, Tojo *et al* received their just deserts, their chief accomplice merely lost his title of God. There is reason to believe that if Russia's alliance had been more soundly based and trustworthy and the Japanese Islands had not been so adjacent to Russia's eastern sphere of influence the Emperor might have paid a much higher price!

The comment has frequently been made that Yamashita, at least, should never have been hanged for his wartime actions, on the grounds that his activities in the field were beyond reproach during the Malayan campaign. Nevertheless, when Singapore was invested by the Japanese in 1942 he gave guarantees that both the armed forces and civilians would be protected. These were never observed as the many organised massacres throughout the occupation prove. Hundreds of Chinese civilians were herded to the eastern part of the island, forced to dig their own graves and executed, largely by bayonet, and a similar fate overtook the Chinese who were machine-gunned in Singapore harbour. Countless numbers of women were raped and assaulted in other ways.

It has to be argued that the commander in the field must be held responsible, regardless of whether his troops take such action without his knowledge or on his orders. Yamashita was well aware of the Japanese soldiers' actions in Nanking and Manchuria and he had no reason to believe that the leopards would change their spots just because they were in Singapore.

It is a strange commentary on the psyche of the Japanese that people who could commit, without hesitation, such atrocities on their fellow-men could be so childishly simple in other respects.

On several occasions throughout our association with the Imperial Japanese Army they indicated that they had received parcels of 'comforts' from home. These were usually of plywood rocking-horses and monkey-up-a-stick gadgets normally associated with toddlers in this country. It was quite amazing to see a crowd of our worst tormentors surrounding the lucky recipient of one of these parcels and laughing with uncontrollable joy at the toys' antics. Likewise, the sweets they received were of the dolly mixture type that any UK man would have seen as an insult. They were consumed with deep satisfaction.

When we worked on the godowns in Singapore prior to leaving for Siam we were approached by the young Japanese officer in charge and told that one of us had to pair with him in a trial of strength where the two men sat on the ground facing each other, putting their heels together, crossing their shins, and one forcing the other's leg to the ground.

As the challenger was wearing leather riding-boots no response was forthcoming, as our own legs were bare. When he finally selected me I felt that honour was at stake, both personal and national. Three times I forced his leg to the ground to the great joy of my compatriots. His eyes filled with tears, he got up disconsolately and walked away. He had undergone that most serious of all degradations: lost the game and lost face to the enemy!

By the end of April 1943, the food improved in quality if not in quantity. The Japanese now began to issue pork to us in the shape of half a pig to 500 men but these were poor little runty things kept on many smallholdings in the Far East and they barely flavoured any of the meals around that time. Most of the cooking was done by traditional Chinese methods in an iron saucer about five feet in diameter, known as a kwali. This allowed the rice to be stirred during cooking, and when the water had evaporated a thin sheet of burnt rice remained on the whole area of the kwali. This usually generated a 'lagi' queue, lagi being the Malayan word for more, and in hungrier times fights took place over the distribution of this delicate morsel.

With the increased workload, the continuous malaria and dysentery and the poor food, the symptoms of beriberi became even more pronounced. The grosser ones fell into either the wet or dry category: in the former the body became increasingly swollen with fluid, starting at the feet and generally working up to the bottom of the rib-cage. This resulted in an absurdly wide-based gait, and acute discomfort in the distended limbs. The latter produced all the appearances of an ambulant cadaver, an impression emphasised by the retracted upper lip. Risus sardonicus indeed! There were other less obvious symptoms: severe loss of memory and concentration, distortion and loss of vision, impaired hearing, and that extremely painful condition known by us as Happy Feet, when men would sit around stamping their feet on the ground in order to lessen the pain. What deadened some nerves heightened the response of others and the condition known as hyperaesthesia was observed in several cases, where the gentle drawing of a feather over the skin caused intolerable pain. Almost all of this was due to the absence of the Vitamin B complex. We had an average age-group of about twenty two, and yet men were dropping dead without a word of warning, or dying in their sleep. The medical opinion was that we were now experiencing the physical standards that we could expect at seventy years of age, but having achieved my biblical span I must record very gratefully that I feel a lot fitter now than I did then. The only therapy supplied by the Japanese was very limited amounts of rice polishings, but experience suggested that these did nothing to remove either the oedema or its cause, tasted foul, and worsened the continuing diarrhoea.

The announcement on parade on 10 April 1943 that twenty-two people had died and forty-eight were acutely ill as a result of cholera at a camp thirty-five miles north of us did nothing to raise our spirits, as we moved rapidly in that direction each day. Cholera is an annual feature of that part of tropical Asia but we were working in an area of scant indigenous population where it might have been expected that the source of infection would be minimal. It was a bad outlook for many hundreds in the up-country area, and for those approaching it from either side. At the CO's request I gave a talk to the camp on water-borne infection and the preventives available in those primitive conditions. As we were now removed from the river when on the line, we drew our water from stagnant pools from which we removed dense green scum and frog spawn. Even when boiled it tasted foul. Our hazards were greatly increased on 1 June with the addition of 500 Thai and Chinese coolies impressed by the Imperial Japanese Army into our camp. They urinated, defaecated, spat and threw food indiscriminately all over the camp, much to the joy of the fly population, and the sorrow of the white population.

The onset of the monsoons in early May was a mixed blessing, for while they certainly washed away the human ordure from the camp, they made the construction of the line, the cuttings, the embankments and the bridges almost impossible. We were now wet for twenty-four hours a day, the sheer volume of water ensuring that what didn't enter the hut through leaking roofs drifted in in the form of spray through the open ends of the hut. At all times we worked ankle-deep in mud, and those who still had the luxury of boots suffered acutely from trench feet. The irritation produced by this is so intense that we never found the person who could resist the temptation to scratch. This very soon peeled off the skin and this left only the raw flesh, with all that meant when working, and the enormous risk of tropical ulcers and amputation, which frequently followed. If the Imperial Japanese Army had had the basic humanity to issue some of the thousands of shirts, shorts and boots left in Singapore – which were largely useless to them – what a lot of suffering could have been saved. When the clothes and boots which we took into captivity in February 1942 had finally worn out through sweat, sun and hard labour, we were issued with a black Jap-Happy – a loin cloth some eighteen by eight inches with tapes attached – by the Japanese – and in my camp at least we were beaten up for being indecently dressed. Thanks to our issue 'housewife', we had now patched the patches until the original material was no longer apparent, and after months of futile endeavour we threw away the remnants, which in any case were warm and reproductive havens for the bugs and lice which were our constant companions.

Like all Europeans we were loath to part with our boots: if we left them in camp they would be stolen either by the Asiatics or the less-scrupulous of our own party, and if we wore them we soon contracted trench feet. By the middle of 1943 most of us had had the problem solved by nature. Now we had to learn to walk through gritty mud, to grip with our toes, and to beware of the accumulating semi-circle of mud on each sleeper, added to by each foot, and particularly where bridges were concerned; only space and water were below.

In early June we came across a team of fifty-four elephants with their Thai mahouts removing teak logs from the jungle to the river. We were fascinated by their intelligence, power and grace, never more so than when they turned to line up the protruding ends of logs with trunks and tusks. Their task was arduous because of the bow-wave of viscous mud created by each log but they leaned their great weight into their harness and bellowed with frustration until it was mobile. I feel that they had never seen track or train, yet they climbed the embankment, tested both sleeper and rail with their trunk, and continued on their graceful way. Whoever coined that stupid phrase, 'As clumsy as an elephant'? I never saw one yet.

On 11 June we transferred to Tarsau camp, and all our worst fears were confirmed. We were now under canvas, the roofs of which were so split and rotten that we slept under a constant cascade of storm-force water; the latrines overflowed, the embankment was frequently washed away, mosquitoes, sandfly and latrine flies infested the entire area.

But these were minor tribulations compared with the fact that we were now firmly in the cholera belt; many had died, many were ill with a variety of intestinal complaints, beriberi and pellagra were increasingly evident, and the poverty of our food was in inverse ratio to the brutality of the Japanese and Koreans.

The greater the pressure from HQ to maintain the tempo of the speedo, the greater the violence in order to muster a working party; and on the track the brutality continued unabated. If a man had a tropical ulcer covering his entire shin that is where he was kicked; and if through the ravages of high temperature and malarial rigor he was not in control of his senses, he was beaten until he collapsed. Yasume breaks were now part of history and meal-times were shortened to the time necessary to eat a bowl of rice. Because of the incessant rain and lack of shelter, the rice was replaced by rain as quickly as it was eaten, and the few dried vegetables in the so-called stew did nothing to titillate the appetite or overcome the beriberi.

By the end of June, in one week we had done one non-stop period of twenty six hours and two of twenty-four hours, in non-stop rain, on the line. We were now delayed by the cliff of solid rock that sloped right across the intended track at Tonchan. Thus was born the hammer-and-tap gang, whose sole effort all day was directed towards drilling as many holes as possible in the rock face to take the charges of dynamite. (The Japanese usually lit the fuses without warning and on one such occasion I was almost taken out of circulation. When I heard the explosion I took shelter behind a small tree, on the other side of which a huge piece was gouged out, level with my head and about fifteen inches away. Many prisoners were injured in this way on the line).

Only the most primitive tools were used – a pointed

crowbar and a hammer – which two men took it in turn to use, one guiding and one hammering. A depth of about one metre was necessary and the number of holes required depended on the size of the obstruction. Once the charge had been detonated the razor-sharp fragments had to be used as ballast, which meant multiple lacerations when carrying the stretchers in our bare feet.

An incident occurred at the Wam Po cutting that clearly illustrated the stupidity of many of the Japanese. A party of four or five had been sent up the cliff face to loosen with crowbars a large boulder which was poised above the track. The Japanese soldier stood immediately below, screaming as usual, 'Speedo, speedo. buggairo', not realising that the men were trying to point out that he was in the direct line of the boulder's path. So eventually they dropped it, and squashed the Japanese flat into the ground. The Japanese subsequently built a small shrine on the spot, and every so often put a small pineapple into a rusty tin to mark the passing of another of Hirohito's heroes. I saw no tears on that occasion.

On 23 June we moved camp once again, this time to Tonchan camp at the 130 kilometre mark. The cholera here was at its worst so far, and deaths were occurring every day, without any attempt at isolation, and a total absence of any form of treatment. I have been told by several doctors that if the Japanese had provided the simplest therapy, a needle, a length of tubing and a saline solution to combat the massive dehydration that occurs in cholera many lives could have been saved. With such a vast reserve of coolies the Japanese just weren't interested, and it certainly cut the cost of feeding.

Each morning, at many of the camps, the pathetic trail of stretcher-bearers with their wizened burdens debouched from the huts and made their way to a primitive burial ground. If a padre were available a short committal service was held; and at one camp a massive pit was built, bodies and timber were put in sandwich fashion to the top, and the whole lot set alight with kerosene generously supplied by our captors. This was the only way to deal with such a vast number of daily deaths.

That beloved physician, the late and great Dr C.E. Vardy,

medical superintendent of Johore Bahru Hospital in peace-time, and largely responsible for the cholera cases in Chungkai POW camp in 1943, gave a talk to a POW club in 1967 at my request and with some diffidence. He quoted what we all knew from experience: that the total dehydration was impossible to combat without some form of medical treatment. He quoted the instance of three Australians from Chungkai cookhouse who went to him at 2300 hours and said that they all had symptoms of cholera. Because they were in the cookhouse they were all of eleven or twelve stones weight. By 0700 hours on the following morning they were all in the five stones region and dead. He said that what distressed him as much as the many deaths he had witnessed were the agonised screams of those whose bones were broken by the muscular contraction of dehydration – and for whom he had no painkillers.

He then sat down and wept – twenty-four years after the main event and after forty years as a doctor in many areas. Such was his compassion.

The Japanese were now so alarmed at the prospects for their wretched railway through the unanticipated mortality that we were ordered to form an anti-cholera squad of four or five men, of which I was one. Our duties mainly consisted of keeping a forty-gallon drum of water at the boil so that mess-tins and spoons could be immersed before and after each meal, and providing a similar container of drinking water. This required the continuous provision of both wood and water when the men were in camp. On one foray into what I took to be the surrounding jungle, I was surprised to hear weak calls for *parni, parni* (water, water). Investigation revealed several dozen Tamils abandoned by the Japanese without food or water, and on the point of death. I hurried back to the camp with my bundle and sought permission to take water to those poor wretches. This was forcefully forbidden because of the cross-migration of both cholera and dysentery. I can still see the wisdom of this but not the humanity.

While on the subject of diseases and their treatment it is perhaps worth recording that most people on the railway had had injections against both cholera and plague by this time, from the Japanese. We suspected with good reason that these were trials by the Japanese of their own products for administration to their troops when they achieved their goal of occupying India. Many of us were made violently ill and physically helpless by these inoculations, and having read of the Japanese experiments on prisoners in their wartime laboratories – major surgery without anaesthetic, injections into eyes and other organs, trials with poisons, gases and germs – one is tempted to believe that it was all part of common ground.

Certainly, Adolf Hitler could teach nothing to the 'Sons of Heaven'.

On 2 July 1943 for reasons that escaped us entirely, we were issued with fifty-five cigarettes, twenty ounces of tinned fish, and small quantities of tinned butter and milk. Only after the war did we learn that, because of the reports reaching the outside world of torture, starvation and death, did the Japanese respond to repeated pressure from the International Red Cross to be allowed to inspect the camps. When the Japanese eventually acceded to this they kitted out the POWs in the smaller camps with British shirts, shorts, hats, socks and boots, and promptly took these away when the visitors left with their photos. Needless to say, no private interviews were allowed. Several camps reported that the Japanese had stolen what goods they wanted and exposed the remainder to the monsoons and bayonet practice.

Throughout the early and middle months of 1943 the Japanese followed yet another back-to-front policy, one that was forced on them by natural processes of weather and physics. The onset of the monsoons had provided the necessary lubricant to the unballasted track to ensure that each loaded train, when going through a curve, pushed the lines off centre. This was particularly dangerous in darkness, and on several occasions trains almost rolled down the embankment. It was easily corrected with the jemmies that we used every day, but obviously couldn't be allowed to continue.

So we now attempted to do what should have been done before the first line was laid: we ballasted the entire track. After months of use the sleepers were buried in the mud of the trace. Truckloads of ballast were used to deposit an appropriate amount between each pair of sleepers, and then the 'ballasty men' took over. Teams of four men were provided with four hammers, each hammer with a three foot haft and teak head, each head being about sixteen inches in length and metal shod on all central surfaces. Two men stood between the rails on a sleeper, and one man on each end of the same sleeper on the outside of the rails. The hammers were enormously heavy to wield all day long, and produced violent pains in our shoulders, backs and hands, the last of which were soon severely blistered. As has previously been noted, many of the sleepers were rotten through long use elsewhere but such was the Japanese poverty of supply that they had to be used.

The Japanese insisted that a perfect rhythm had to be maintained by all four men, and quite violent beatings were administered when (a) the rhythm was broken, (b) the sleeper was splintered, (c) the ballast wasn't driven smoothly under the sleeper and evenly throughout its entire length. The little coolie who supervised us never knew how near he came to having the hammer buried in his head. This work continued until I moved further north to continue with line-laying.

On 6 July there commenced one of the bitterest episodes of my entire captivity. The Japanese demanded a party of seven men, all of whom must be WOs or NCOs and fit enough for arduous work. This provided all concerned with something of a dilemma, even without the limits imposed by rank. Eventually, on a very empirical basis, we mustered two WOs, two sergeants, one bombadier, one gunner and myself. We were known as the Suicide Gang, a name given by the Japanese at the commencement because of their recognition of the dangers involved.

We joined and shared a tent with five Dutchmen at Tonchan Central station. They and their captors had been on site for several days; the Dutchmen were to cook for both the Japanese and ourselves. With typical Japanese foresight we had been issued with no rations and thus had to rely on the crumbs that fell from the rich man's table – little from the Dutch and none from the Japanese. We returned to the Lucullan indulgence of our own rice issue in a day or two.

We formed what can best be described as a mini

marshalling-yard, transporting the rails and sleepers from the supply base to rail-head. We were to work twenty-four hours per day and seven days a week until the line was completed. As a fairly lengthy journey was involved in each direction, and as we were well aware, by this time, of the Japanese inability to schedule any journey, we decided that whoever went south would break his journey here on the way north; and vice versa those who went north would hand over the empty train here on the way back. The major problem now was that we were working through the mountains on the Burma/Siam border and what had proved adequate traction on the plains of Siam was now totally inadequate for mountain-climbing. In addition, we were now paying the price for the months of neglect of both lorries and bogies. Where brakes had fallen off they had been thrown on the track-side, links that connected empty bogies in pairs had been lost, couplings that joined 'trucks' to each other had broken and been replaced in many cases by single strands of galvanised wire. Lights and horns no longer worked so it was impossible to signal for brake assistance where this was available, and the diesel lorries were at their last gasp.

The nightmare that had pursued us throughout the construction of the line now assumed much greater proportions. It had always been the practice for the diesel to push the load to rail-head and it was then free to return to base for the next load of eight or ten 'trucks'. Where, as so often happened, the load was on a slope, gravity would set it silently in motion, and it was usually possible to apply brakes or chock wheels with sleepers, and for those on the train to jump off. Where steep mountains were concerned these options were rarely feasible; and if the diesel broke down or one of the trucks broke free the combination of weight, gravity, wet wheels and wet rails ensured a rapid and terrifying return to the starting point. This only once happened to me, I am grateful to say.

The historiographers of the line record that there was one bridge or culvert per kilometre in the 263 kilometres from Non Pladuk to Three Pagoda Pass. This involved the small crossings of streams and chasms, as well as the major bridges of Hintok, Wam Po, and the Mae Khlong (Kwai).

91

With the exception of the last, all these bridges were built of raw wood from the jungle, and there wasn't a nut and bolt in one of them. They were fastened by gigantic staples driven into two adjoining wood surfaces, and where great height and wind were concerned they were dangerously unstable, bearing in mind that they were built to carry fully-laden troop trains, drawn by steam engines. (The Hintok bridge collapsed three times during construction, and was pulled upright by elephant: we subsequently crossed it every day by train). The northern section of the line from Three Pagoda Pass to Thanbuzayat was 113 kilometres in length and was similarly bridged.

Now that we were working in the mountains we crossed several of these structures on each journey, and there was one large one on the northern track immediately beyond our present camp. Each Japanese driver left the station at breakneck speed to make sure that he reached his destination without stopping, for reasons already explained. What was frightening by day became terrifying by night to everyone involved. It was frequently pouring with monsoon rain, the diesel engine was running at maximum decibels, and we were in total darkness. We knew from daytime experience that as we snaked up the mountain we were shedding sleepers and boxes of fishplates through centrifugal force, and where there was occasional starlight we could see this reflected in the wet wood as it disappeared. Most of these items were never recovered as they disappeared into abysses that were a hundred feet or more deep, and frequently carrying cataracts of great force. The return journey was equally threatening as the empty bogies, brakeless and wired together, cavorted about on the wet rails.

On 9 July 1943 the promised tragedy occurred. A battery sergeant major, with whom I had struck up a warm friendship, took the early morning trip south and I was due to take the load from him on his return. The line was twenty to thirty yards from my tent, and as I heard the train returning I collected my mess-tin and ran from the tent. For once it was a beautifully sunny morning and as I approached he called to me that he would continue to the rail-head and I could take the next train south on his return.

The train left us at the usual breakneck speed, and some fifty seconds later we heard a violent crash that signalled the end of that trip. A friend and I followed the usual practice of hacking the two inner corners off two rice bags, with spades, grabbing two stout bamboos, and running to the scene.

Of all the many accidents we had seen to date, this was by far the worst. Immediately over the wooden bridge several dozen slabs of what appeared to be slate had been blasted out and then stood vertically with many points and razor edges at the top. The diesel remained on the rails but the rest had overturned onto the slate, smudging my friend along the entire surface, and it was apparent that he hadn't long to live: the base of his skull was fractured and his brain escaping, left ear torn off, chest stove in, scrotum torn open, two cuts to the bone left thigh, a deep laceration in the left kidney region, and multiple lacerations all over, with profuse overall bleeding.

As usual, the Japanese was more interested in his train and load than in the victim. As we were apparently in virgin jungle I ran down a small track in the hope that I could find a kampong whose inhabitants would help us to carry the BSM back to our tent, when we would arrange a train to take him to our MOs. By one of those miracles I met two Dutch doctors whom I knew well and told them what had happened. The younger ran back to the camp to prepare the reception, and the elder came to see the patient. He was still bleeding profusely, having short periods of rational consciousness, and then lapsing into deep unconsciousness.

He died on 10 July at 2200, and on 11 July we formed a burial party and carried him to one of the all-too-familiar cemeteries hacked out of the edge of the jungle. His shroud was the bloody rice-bags on which we had carried him to camp two days previously. And there, but for the grace of God, went I.

For some reason that we never fathomed the Japanese stopped all operations for three days and we assumed that this was out of concern for their personnel and rolling stock – and then the speedo took off again at a compensatory level.

93

Over the four days following the accident, three of the remaining six men were returned to camp with severe dysentery and one other was so badly beaten up that he was unable to work. Even the Japanese had to admit that the two of us could no longer sustain such a punishing effort and as I still had diarrhoea I was only too glad to leave. We re-joined our unit at Tam Pei (150 kilometres mark) on 18 July.

It is worth recording an interesting episode that occurred while on the suicide job. After the BSM's death we were allowed to travel on the back of the lorry instead of on the bogies and on this occasion I shared the space with a Japanese private. This was surprising as such people usually shared the cab with the driver. The journey was undertaken late at night and in solid monsoon rain.

Speaking in perfect idiomatic and grammatical English he told me that his father was Japanese and his mother Australian, and she had insisted that he learn English. He asked me what I thought of the Japanese and I replied that, as I had seen so many thousand acts of violence and he had a rifle and bayonet, I would be a fool to answer. He promised that there would be no retribution so I took him at his word and told him that they were a nation of sadistic bullies, relied on their rifle and bayonet, and that if we were face to face on equal terms we would beat the daylights out of them. He said, quietly, 'Yes, I agree with you,' and when we reached rail-head he brought me a mug of tea.

Conditions at Tam Pei were as disgusting as any we had had to date. Thanks to the almost incessant rain and endemic diarrhoea the latrines were full to the top, and the area surrounding them was covered with moving maggots to a circumference at about five feet. It was impossible to use the latrine without standing on them as the ground was completely covered. The position was even worse at night-time as there were no wooden slats to protect against the undermined sides collapsing, it was pitch dark and at all times we were in bare feet covered with mud. I know of several men who fell in at least part of the way but we never knew of one drowning.

From all viewpoints, conditions were at their worst yet. In order to sustain the speedo we were obliged to work in twenty-four and thirty-six hour shifts, and as this irritated the Japanese as much as it did us, the rifle butts and teaksticks were liberally applied, and we were encouraged at frequent intervals with demoniacal screams of 'Speedo, speedo'. Almost every man now had trench foot and deep lacerations to the soles and sides of the feet. We walked as do cats on hot bricks and when we returned to camp we collapsed on our buggy and lousy beds, and although water was frequently cascading onto us through numerous holes, we were asleep instantly – until the Japanese were beating our raw feet with their sticks at the start of another day.

Wherever we went the story was the same. Because of our mobility we passed through working parties from static camps to the north of us. As has been said, they lacked the line as a means of supply until we reached them, and they had suffered more than we had through inadequate food, a total lack of all forms of medication, and the invasions of cholera, dysentery, malaria, dengue and severe starvation. Throughout the hot pre-monsoon season the Japanese had blamed the lack of supplies on the inability of the pom-poms (the native motor boats that supplied the camps), to cope with the too-shallow river; and now of course the opposite would be blamed: too much water for the power of the pom-poms! Soon the cemeteries hacked out of the jungle verges were filling rapidly, and men died because they no longer wanted to live. In one camp a Japanese sergeant tormented his captives until they lay in wait for him, beat him to death and dumped his body in the latrine. They awaited the dawn with apprehension, but the parade passed in the normal way. His absence was not referred to and it was assumed that the Japanese thought that he had deserted. In another camp a similar bully was given a diet of amoebic dysentery faeces with his rice and obliged by dying in agony some days later. It isn't necessary to choke cats with cream on every occasion.

The other evidence of the great speedo was abundant in many places on the side of the line. The Japanese continued to bring thousands of men, women and children from Malaya and Singapore to Siam, encouraging them with promises of a new life, and then dumping them at the side of the line, without food, water, or the means to build shelters or latrines. Most of them were Tamils, never the most provident or independent of people, and they totally lacked the means to survive. Soon the aerial circus of vultures would be seen, and those oriental scavengers would be down prospecting their victims, both alive and dead. When they left, gorged to capacity, only the torn and bloody dhotis marked the completion of yet another tragedy. It is calculated that 140,000 died in this way.

Some of them set out to find food and water for their families and collapsed before they achieved their goal. When they died they began to decompose immediately; their bellies swelled to enormous proportions and finally exploded with a noise like a gun.

On 30 July one of my friends in my tent of ten people went down with cholera. He was moved to another camp, but we merely burned the already torn and rotten tent, washed our hands in disinfectant and continued to mix with the rest of the camp.

Also on 30 July we moved to Kin Sioke camp – yet another clearing on the edge of virgin jungle, and after over two months of monsoon rain a total quagmire. The latrines were overflowing, there was a covering of mud throughout the area to a depth of eight or nine inches, all the tents leaked, the bamboo beds were infected with bugs, and the food was the worst yet in both quantity and quality. As we had moved away from the area where attap huts of a semi-permanent nature had been built we no longer had cover for the immediate need to prepare food two or three times per day. The cookhouse staff of two or three men worked miracles in rigging temporary shelters for the limited stocks of rice and dried vegetables, and, when it came to cooking these goodies, either the volume of water frustrated all attempts to light a fire, or the kwali became full of rain and had to be baled out by the cooks – no easy task when the rice paddle is a beast's thigh-bone and your beaker is one cell of a fully-grown bamboo. As rain continued for days and nights the results would hardly have qualified for inclusion in Mrs Beeton's celebrated volume.

The river was only 150 yards away so we were able to bathe at the end of each shift but it was at the base of an almost vertical cliff, so a rope was necessary in order to transport water for cooking. When we turned in on one occasion we noted that the rope was exactly touching the water. On the following morning we saw that the river had risen considerably so we pulled up the rope and found that, overnight, in a river of 150 yards wide, (using a six foot man's arm-span as a guide), the water had risen ten feet between 2200 and 0600 hours.

In those conditions we were building a speedo railway. Where cuttings had been badly surveyed by the Japanese and had filled with water the sleepers floated away as we tried to lay them; and where the sleepers were waterlogged they sank. The sides of cuttings were undermined and collapsed, embankments were washed away, brakeless trains ran away and shed their loads, and all the time the Japanese kept up their demonic screamings and beatings. If the workers average weight at that time was eight to nine stones, that may be a generous assessment, and everyone had some disease or deficiency, some of them not to be diagnosed until after the war. Diarrhoea, malaria, amoebic and bacillary dysentery, beriberi, pellagra and the immensely painful trench feet were the commonest.

We worked at that time from 0600 hours on one day to 1100 hours on the following: twenty-nine hours almost non-stop, with three pints of rice in the entire period, and perhaps no more than one break of ten minutes every five or six hours. We preferred to keep working in order to sustain warmth as we were naked apart from our loin-cloths and the jungle in that season becomes a natural refrigerator. It was, of course, impossible to light a cigarette in that volume of water.

The pathetic carbide lights that the Japanese had issued when overnight working commenced had long since been discarded. They were the small hand-held variety, did nothing to dispel the encircling gloom, were always deficient in either carbide or water, and were awkward to carry when working. This meant that we had laid the sleepers and rails, fastened the fishplates, discarded the bogies and crossed the bridges by Braille for at least twelve or thirteen hours in each shift, no mean feat when one remembers that on most of the bridges the men's heels overhung deep chasms and rushing water, and lateral pressure with the feet ensured the sleeper's turning sideways, as it was never fastened to the main baulk on which it rested.

By such processes were laid the foundations of premature deaths, and of the chronic ill-health, chronic depression, blindness and deafness that were to become all too apparent in later years.

On 2 August, on returning from the line, I was appointed battalion and brigade clerk, to replace the colour-sergeant and sergeant who had previously done the work and were now in hospital. This silly title – there were no such military demarcations – covered a job that was merely an attempt to tally the workers and list the dead, the latter now having reached alarming proportions throughout Siam. The Japanese were still attempting to do what a blind kitten could have told them was impossible – honour their promise to the Emperor to complete the line to Rangoon by mid-August. I worked for twelve to fourteen hours per day – often by guttering oil-lamp – and enjoyed the mental stimulus after eighteen months of cerebral inertia.

We all recognised that it couldn't last for long and on 21 August I was returned to railway duties along with the anti-cholera men and everyone else who was warm and breathing, despite the fact that we continued to have cholera deaths in the camp. And each day in transit to railhead and back, we passed the thousands of coolies, mainly Chinese and Tamils, who continued to be brought up-country with their wives and children, and who were dumped on the side of the line without food, water, medicine or pity. Disease, ants and the vultures attacked them with gratitude – ante mortem and post mortem. No surer way exists of spreading the waterborne disease of cholera than by putting thousands of improvident and helpless natives up-river of the principal centres of habitation. They were, of course, in the same position as the workers on the line: in the absence of latrines they had no alternative than to move to the first available piece of open ground and squat. This and the torrential rain then ensured the widest possible dissemination of the result; and in the two areas this happened many hundreds of times per day. On more than one occasion the pressures of diarrhoea resulted in a man being caught short and unintentionally defaecating on the side of the line. This provided a welcome opportunity for the nearest Japanese soldier to beat the offender for insulting Hirohito by fouling his line.

On 20 August we had a surprise 'presento' of 167 Javanese cigarettes per man, and a tin of condensed milk to each four men, with margarine and tea sent to the cookhouse for the communal pot. We found the Javanese flavour rather harsh but as we hadn't had any real cigarettes for some months they were very welcome. Non-smokers traded their issue for money or some other commodity. By this time, most of us had accepted that if we were to survive we must concentrate on the essentials of survival, and regarded cigarettes as outside this imperative.

However, those who were heavily addicted suffered severely, and they went to amazing lengths to alleviate that suffering. On the rare occasions that tea was issued the cookhouse made three or four infusions and then gave the remains to the addicted smokers. Leaves, of questionable and possibly harmful cultivation, were cut from the jungle trees, dried, and chopped, and in many cases smoked with blissful pleasure. The associated problem was, of course, paper. By this time, many books had been used for purposes not intended by their authors and publishers, and many had been discarded by exhausted travellers on forced marches, or reduced to papier mâché by the monsoon rain. Bibles, because of their rice paper, were most in demand and the price per sheet would have gone out of the roof in any Stock Exchange quotation; and even the padres recommended this process where it was felt that the material value outweighed the spiritual.

A commodity that supplemented both our diet and our smoking throughout our time in Siam was Ghula Malacca, a brown, viscous and sweet substance that made a tremendous difference to the insipid and inevitable rice. It was described to us as the exudate left over in the refining of sugar.

The Siamese produced a type of cheap tobacco that appeared to be the veins and stalks of the plant, the leaf having been used in the preparation of cigarettes. This could be purchased in lampangs (cushions) of varying size and was guaranteed to paralyse breathing and induce vomiting if smoked untreated. It had to be washed and squeezed very thoroughly, mixed with a watery solution of Ghula Malacca, and then dried as slowly as possible out of the sun. If no paper were available a 'cob' type of pipe could be made from bamboo. Such smokers, dressed in their rags and tatters, looked for all the world like a clip from a Hillbilly film.

On 18 August we moved to Pran Kassi where there wasn't sufficient space to erect our tatty tents, and we had to clear an area for ourselves in the usual torrential rain. The small meat issue continued for the evening meals and was now accompanied by dried vegetable which was cooked on the spot but it had a disgusting taste and was probably of low nutritional value. It certainly took most of the blame for the increase in diarrhoea throughout the camp.

The long overnight shifts continued and these, combined with deteriorating equipment and the weakness and ill-health of all those involved, produced a further increase in accidents on the line. My diary at that time records that these mainly involved derailments and people falling between sleepers on bridges because of the mud deposited by passing feet.

An additional hazard was that posed by an unexpected train when we were halfway across a completed bridge on foot, and particularly in darkness. Long experience had taught us to lower ourselves between the sleepers and rest our feet on the lower struts while the train passed overhead. At least one Japanese detachment was not so lucky, and, lumbered with all the things that the world's armies hang on soldiers, were swept to their deaths.

As has already been noted, all the wooden bridges were completed with two enormous baulks of timber in parallel over their entire length, across which the sleepers were laid. On one such bridge – possibly Hintok – one of these baulks had broken, with the result that each truck took a really frightening dip to one side as it passed, relying on the adjacent trucks to hold it on the line. The most upsetting part of this twice-daily journey was that far below were the remains of an entire train – including, for a time, our comrades who had gone over with it.

100

On 23 September 1943 we moved to Tomajo at the 239 kilometre mark from Non Pladuk. After a short dry spell the rains recommenced and the new camp reverted to type and became the customary mudbath. The river continued to supply its quota of human and animal corpses, shacks and wrecked boats and the flotsam from its passage between jungle banks. The Japanese continued to force onto the line all those who could stand, and usually employed the lowest ranks of their army to make the decision, their authority having been underwritten by rifle butts. Occasionally we were visited by Japanese who claimed to be doctors, but one didn't have to be hospital-trained to realise that they were usually imposters. Indeed we had one Son of Heaven who clearly was a doctor, and who enquired of each FEPOW, in English, 'How are you?' and being given the answer, 'not very well; in pain', etc., would say, 'Good, I hope you die!' To which one FEPOW is reported to have replied, 'And if I do, I'll come back and . . . well haunt you.'

From 4 to 10 October I was detailed to carry a medical bag again, not because of humanity by the Japanese but simply to keep as many men as possible at work. In this I was nothing loath as my trench feet were badly lacerated through walking on ballasting again; and in addition, with my sparse supplies of disinfectant, eusol and mercurochrome I was able to help the Chinese, Tamil, and Malayan coolies and their families. It was a pathetic contribution as there was so much more I could have done with cotton wool, bandages, quinine and so on. They were all grossly emaciated and their death rate still very high. It was reported that of 4,000 coolies who had come to an adjacent camp recently 1,000 had already died of cholera and dysentery.

On 13 October 1943 I received two letters from home dated 17 September 1942 and 6 October 1942 – my third and fourth letters since captivity commenced, and both over a year old. At least everything was well and the family was intact at the time of writing. There was a cornucopia at this time as we were issued with seventy-one cigarettes and a two ounce tin of milk per man, with the usual tea and margarine to the cookhouse; and on the 15th we had been allowed to send a card home with the usual rubbish that we

101

were well and working for pay. One or two added a postscript 'Please let my friends in the Marines know' – a message far too arcane for the Japanese to recognize.

On 16 October 1943 we had our usual early breakfast of rice pap – rice boiled until the grains burst, and forming a watery gruel – and set out once more for the line. Between 1115 hours on 16 October and 0800 hours on 17 October we laid seventy-two trucks – a record for all time. Shortly before midnight on 16 October a Japanese private brought a bucket of cold water into which he measured *two level dessert spoons* of white sugar, stirred it, and told me to issue it to all the men, indicating with the recognised pointing to his biceps that this was to give the men energy. I duly obliged.

The reason for this great beneficence became apparent a little later when a signals officer, whom I had known for some years, told me that he had been around the corner, and had seen a working party coming towards us. Knowing that the Japanese had injured his jaw, broken his teeth and burst a kidney with a rifle butt, and that he was as tired as I was, I made no more than a perfunctory acknowledgement as I felt that he might have become unhinged by his suffering.

He was correct, of course. This was the first we had heard of the party working south on the much smaller section from Thanbuzayat in Burma, and when we had worked around the cliff-face, there they were on the trace below, looking like so many fireflies as they were still using the carbide lamps, and we could hear their voices and the rhythm of their hammers.

For the concluding session of joining the two sets of line the Japanese were foolish enough to challenge us to a race. They used soldiers who worked on the good old military foundation of one-two, one-two. We used eleven months of hard experience. Their idea was that we should lay four trucks each but when the Japanese major who sat on our truck saw that they were losing handsomely, despite his beating us over the head and knuckles with his teak stick, he declared the race null and void, and substituted another race of eleven rails each. I had the exquisite pleasure of pushing from top to bottom of a high embankment a Japanese soldier who got in my way. By the time we had completed our eleven rails the Japanese soldiers were struggling with their seventh, and it was thus declared no contest, with typical Japanese sportsmanship.

The line was declared open when diesel lorries approaching from each side met at the point of union at the 262.80 kilometre mark. Films and photos were taken of the ceremony, lasting one-and-a-half hours and accompanied by an excellent Japanese military band.

On 17 October 1943 at 1700 hours, we arrived back at Tomajo after thirty four hours of non-stop work, four bowls of rice, and a few grains of sugar in a pint of water!

The major task of captivity was complete; and as a token of their appreciation of our efforts our Imperial hosts gave each man half of a very small tin of sardines, and half a day's holiday.

But we had a final act to perform in that enormous tragedy, a concluding torture and murder that epitomised their love of cruelty.

When the camp was near to a river it was the custom to put our mess-tins in our bedspace when we returned from work, and to bath before dinner. As I had moved into a new hut in Tomajo on the previous day I saw nothing amiss in the absence of my immediate neighbour's mess-tin, assuming either that he had not yet come in or had gone straight to the river.

However, on my return from the river neither he nor his mess-tin was there, and I started to make enquiries. His friend then told me what had happened.

On our return journey after the completion of the line on that day the diesel truck pulling our train had almost run out of fuel, and we had been dropped off in a jungle clearing while the driver went to fill his tank. The missing soldier had had a malarial rigor at midday with high temperature and irrational behaviour.

When last seen he was soundly asleep. When the diesel returned we were all so exhausted that we had climbed aboard and paid little heed to those around us. It was now realised that he had been left behind.

The Japanese were asked to provide an escort to allow the POWs to retrace the afternoon journey and, as anticipated, they flatly refused. After reporting that the man was in urgent need of medical help, and employing some verbal pressure, they agreed to provide one armed soldier and to allow a small number of captives to pursue the search – on foot; no train would be provided.

So these exhausted, sick and hungry men set off. When they reached the clearing some miles north there was no sign of the missing man, and as the trace was the only route that he could have taken they prevailed on the escort to continue northwards, assuming that in his dazed condition the missing man had turned north on leaving the clearing.

When they reached a Japanese engineers' camp they asked the escort to enquire after the POW, and shortly afterwards he reported that their journey was at an end, and they were taken into the camp. Our friend was lying dead at the foot of a tree.

The manner of his death was agonisingly obvious to all who knew the working of the Japanese mind. He had been suspended over a branch of a tree by a rope tied to his thumbs and with his feet clear of the ground. His torturers had then danced around him, burning his body with cigarettes and punching and beating him; they had then cut him down while still alive and given the coup de grace by taking it in turns to kick him to death.

Their excuse was that they thought he was a spy: acutely ill, eight stones in weight, bare-footed and wearing an issue Jap-happy!

5

BRUTES AND MEN

History shows that we had now completed twenty months of our forty-two months of captivity, and this may be as good a place as any to make some comments of a general nature, particularly on those aspects of our experience that were with us throughout that time.

Few of us who knew the Japanese well would have believed him capable of planning and executing the world-wide industrial expansion of the post-war years. He was an ardent copyist and blue-print thief, and all of us saw the evidence of this. The bicycles on which the Japanese cycled down Malaya during the campaign were all Raleighs – with the famous emblems of the crane on the lamp-holder, and the circular fork-crowns. They bore the Raleigh motif and the words 'made in Nottingham', and in miniscule underneath 'Osaka'.

But, apart from a few Japanese officers who were obviously well-educated and qualified, the Japanese and Korean soldiers appeared to be sub-normal to the point of stupidity. Their repeated efforts to count three rows of twenty men per row had to be seen to be believed. When trains were slowing through lack of power we were forced to help the engine by putting our hands on the truck's side and pushing; the more we grunted and stamped our feet the happier they were, but we were *inside* the truck; and I understand from my nautical friends that the same dynamics were applied at sea to make ships go faster.

In Singapore I saw a Japanese sergeant, who had obviously never driven a vehicle, run a Light Aid Detachment lorry off the road. There is a small crane on the back of such vehicles for recovery purposes; and the Japanese took the hook of this, fastened it under the axle of the same vehicle, and swore like the proverbial trooper because it wouldn't lift itself out of the ditch.

In Singapore, British drivers drew several gallons of petrol per day for their steamrollers, took it round the corner and sold it to the eager Chinese. The Japanese never learnt that steamrollers don't run on petrol.

So far as propaganda was concerned our captors were childishly credulous. They had obviously been conditioned to think that they were on the final lap of conquering India, and on detraining from the troop trains that were now able to get to Burma would eagerly enquire 'This India?', and 'This Burma?' We took a fiendish delight in drawing the relative maps on th ground with sticks, and locating a very southern point in a very long Siam.

Both the papers printed in the Japanese script and the *Syonan Times*, (ex *Straits Times*) carried quite dramatic stories of the courage and ingenuity of their servicemen. Pilots regularly flew their fighters upside down, opened their canopies, drew their swords, and beheaded admirals standing on their bridges; and an invasion task-force of the enemy was forced to retreat when vigorously bombarded with rice-balls by the courageous Japanese.

There is, of course, a clearly discernible relationship between the Bushido approach to duty and death in wartime and an equally dedicated approach to the work ethic in peace-time. The Japanese servicemen were encouraged to believe that if they died in battle they would be enshrined as gods in the Yasukuni Shrine in Tokyo. It is hard to say whether this lay behind their utterly pointless self-sacrifice in many battles when they attacked an unassailable target in waves which piled corpse upon corpse and achieved nothing. One such site in Singapore was reported to have a wall of corpses twelve feet high. Western armies learnt long ago that it is better to retire and live to fight another day.

The Japanese do not commit hara kiri in the face of defeat, of course. Many, many thousands with the means to shoot or disembowel themselves, quite happily and gratefully surrendered to the Allied forces, many of the most brutal of our immediate captors grovelling with pieces of

106

paper requesting our testimony to their kindness.

There is a clear association between this military attitude and the approach to industrial dedication: keep your nose to the grindstone, your feet on the treadmill, your hand to the plough and all will be well with the motherland, and its capitalists; and by lies, dissimulation and broken promises of fair trading they have made it so. A recent report stated that the average Japanese worker took six days holiday a year, so the events of the battlefield may be equated with the events of the factory floor.

The more that successive prime ministers of Japan attempt to re-write history and eliminate their appalling wartime record from their schools' curriculum, the more the world recalls their atrocities. They were never magnanimous in victory, either to the inhabitants of the countries they occupied or to the enemy, and they introduced a reign of terrorism and suppression in every sphere.

Their arrogance led them to insist that everyone, friend and foe alike, should bow to everything Japanese and address men as San (Mr). This stuck in the gullet of most of us, of course, and we did everything possible to avoid such confrontations. The Japanese soldier, ever conscious of the need to maintain face and boost his ego, adopted many stratagems to outwit us. The favourite was to hide behind trees, particularly during the hours of darkness, and await his oblivious victim. Apologies were not part of the game: only the rifle-butt, the fist and the boot could requite such wrongs.

One of the severer punishments meted out, often for trivial or non-existent reasons, was to make the victim stand in the blazing sunshine with a boulder over his head. Even a fit man finds this an impossible feat for more than a minute of so. Starvation, illness and hard labour ensured that it was beyond the capacity of even the fittest of the captives. Dropping it resulted in injury to the head, face and feet, and a severe beating from one or more Japanese. The process was then repeated, and the victim kept without food or water for twenty-four or forty-eight hours, until he collapsed. Only then could he be removed to a more humane and civilised community.

The late Major Murdoch Mackenzie, R.A. told a most

illuminating story concerning a Japanese senior officer who wished to be taught French. Thinking that this might help his men and create good relations he agreed to be the tutor. Whenever he visited the Japanese tent he was delighted to see that a kitten played around the pupil's feet, jumped on his lap and sat on his shoulders – the only evidence that Sandy Mackenzie had ever seen of a Japanese being kind to a dumb animal. After several lessons and on a very hot evening the Japanese officer suggested that they should go outside and cool down at the edge of a waterfall on the camp boundary, and the kitten went with them and played around their feet.

Without warning, the Japanese hooked his boot under the kitten, and cast it over the cliff into the turbulent water. To Sandy's question, 'Why on earth did you do that?' the Japanese said, 'I just wanted to see what happened.' Whereupon Sandy replied, 'I will never teach you another lesson,' about-turned, and never went back.

The Japanese, for a nation that prided itself so deeply on decorum and saving face, had some peculiar ideas on what constituted dignity. The officers usually wore a shapeless, soft-peaked cap and a very smart silk shirt with a well-fitting green jacket, and on most of our *tenkos* (parades), they wore a dress sword which, because of the wearer's lack of height, had to be forced into the horizontal position by keeping the hand on the hilt. What appeared below the waist seemed to be of small concern to most of the officers: riding breeches, with the calf laces hanging loose, wooden choplis instead of boots, ankle socks – or alternatively white cotton pyjamas replacing those items. If their hands were occupied, the sword was allowed to trail along the ground.

Many of them carried what used to be called, in the old days of cavalry, a sabretache, a beautiful leather 'brief-case', for maps and orders, and hanging from a waist-belt. Again, lack of height meant that this usually ended by banging on the wearer's knees.

In either case, the result always looked like a comedian parodying command, and caused all of us endless mirth; the more so as most Japanese are slightly bandy-legged, and walk with their feet pointing to the ten-to-two position, as on the clock face.

Larger contingents of the Japanese army were usually accompanied by what is known universally as camp followers – a euphemism in many cases for prostitutes. These were obviously hand-picked, not for beauty but for total and repellent ugliness, as thought the High Command were saying, 'If you must do this, we will discourage you as much as possible.' They were usually grossly fat and hirsute, without the slightest claim to muliebrity, and would have made a sensitive man dedicate himself to a life of celibacy.

☆   ☆   ☆

It would be foolish to pretend that the POWs were examples of all that was good and true in life, whatever their country of origin. We had rogues who tried to sell other people's property – blankets, razors, clothes (in the earlier days), and watches – but at least it may be said in their defence that they were starving, and were usually seeking the means to buy food. In any case, such incidents were few and far between, and only three cases spring to my mind in the entire POW experience.

There are, of course, many other ways of failing to observe a decent code of behaviour in such austere circumstances: selfishness, being Jap-happy (not the garment but being ingratiating and helpful to the Japanese – a very rare condition), selling to your fellow captives at exorbitant prices, dodging work or claiming non-existent sickness.

Except in the latter part of the speedo our officers went out on working parties only one day at a time and usually only in a supervisory capacity; and because they were in charge they took many violent and disabling beatings. Many of them showed great courage and refused to be defeated by violence; and they persisted in their efforts to obtain better accommodation, more food and medical supplies and a lessening of work hours.

However, not all of them were so highly motivated. We had a padre who wore his Red Cross brassard permanently, spent his entire up-country life inside his hut/tent reading, and was reported to have several shirts, slacks, boots and shoes which he firmly refused to share with anyone, and all of which had to be transported by others in our many moves up and down the railway camps. He was a remote figure to all of us and I cannot recall his ever holding a service or visiting the sick and dying.

We had a medical officer who, when the death rates were at their highest in Siam, issued ticals in exchange for promissory notes to an equal number of pounds sterling, and payable at the end of the war. This despicable usury would have earned him a profit of more than 90 per cent. He was called before his colonel and used the usual excuse that he was doing it as an act of generosity to his fellows. The colonel ordered him to destroy the IOUs immediately on pain of being reported to the General Medical Council after the war. He complied.

We knew that this practice was being conducted at the time, and it was the colonel concerned who gave me the final details after the war. He was, of course, highly contemptuous of the MO involved.

On the whole, the POWs of all nationalities mixed well, and there was little real friction. We were always touched by the generosity of the Dutch, who included us in the celebration of their Queen's birthday. This usually involved burnt-rice coffee and small tapioca-flour cakes, all paid for by the Dutch. We persisted in concluding with the Dutch and British national anthems, as a means of driving the Japanese into paroxysmal rage as well as demonstrating our patriotism.

Regimental esprit de corps played a major part in boosting morale, beating the Japanese by a show of spirit, and maintaining the process of interdependence. In this, no greater effort was made than by the Royal Northumberland Fusiliers, backed up, of course, by the innate friendliness of the Geordie, born of years of hardship in the industrial north and the great depression of the thirties.

Above all were the individual friendships and the small groups of dedicated cobbers. By pooling resources and sharing windfalls we were able to ensure that those involved gained some benefit from whatever was available. If a man worked in the Japanese cookhouse and obtained some extra food as a 'presento' he shared it with the others. Similarly, loads were carried on the long marches for sick and weak members, food – the inevitable rice – was fed to convalescent people too weak or disoriented to feed themselves, men whose injuries had involved their hands and arms were bathed and shaved, and precious clothes were sold in order to buy food for the many victims caused by a Japanese-created famine.

It is worth repeating that no such spirit was discernible in the Japanese forces. If there was such a thing as camaraderie or personal friendship among the Japanese it was conspicuous by its absence, and even in times of dire need they appeared to be loath to see to each other's needs.

Every POW has been asked in the post-war years why, if things were so bad, he didn't try to escape. Most of the reasons are self-evident:

(1) Europeans stuck out more conspicuously than a sore thumb because of their colouring, both of hair and skin, and their height.

(2) Singapore Island was so small that Europeans were immediately obvious, and the Japanese ubiquitous. Even a small boat, fully provisioned, could only have travelled as far as other Japanese-occupied territory.

(3) For most of the time in Siam we were barricaded in by virgin jungle through which there were no tracks through Burma to the coast and the Indian Ocean.

(4) The transportation of sufficient food, the lighting of fires for cooking, and the constant threat of illness, made such a project totally hazardous, even in the dry season.

(5) Every POW had a price on his head, which many of the indigenous population were very happy to collect.

(6) Several men did attempt to escape. Almost all of them were re-captured and were summarily shot, decapitated or used as bayonet dummies – after digging their own graves.

Many Japanese are of Buddhist persuasion. One of the principal tenets of this religion is that all life is sacred!

6

BUNDS, BOMBS AND BOLTHOLES

Any expectation we had that the completion of the line would result in the lessening of our labours or a period of rest and convalescence proved vain. The Japanese celebrated the event by giving us half a tin of sardines per man and half a day's holiday.

Such days, particularly now that the monsoons were over, were put to good use. The return of the hot weather allowed us to debug and delouse our blankets, Jap-happies and rice-bags. If the Japanese could find a chore for us on such yasume days they always did so: unloading rice-trains, re-railing derailed trains, chopping wood for the cookhouse fires, etc. If we were left in peace we could read, chat, shave, and, where appropriate, write up our forbidden diaries.

Major Lees, Argyll and Sutherland Highlanders, was currently our CO and he was so concerned about the state of the men under his command that a nominal roll was raised of the present strength. He found that of the 600 who had commenced work on the line ten months previously only 100 remained on 17 October. The remainder were either dead or had been evacuated down-country with dysentery, malaria, tropical ulcers and injuries sustained at work. He issued a certificate in writing to each of us as a mark of his appreciation, and mine is treasured not only as a memento of that effort but of a great and gentle man who was honoured and respected by all of us.

Now that troop-trains were pulled by continental-type woodburning engines it was necessary to have large stocks of wood stacked at the side of the line throughout Siam and Burma, and this was now our regular job, as troops and supplies were frequently going up-country.

112

The maintenance of the line was of prime importance to the Japanese as a breakdown at any point put the entire system out of use. Despite the supervision of the Japanese and the realisation that we might become the first victims of our own handiwork, we had managed to build several booby-traps into the trace – mainly bamboo cages which formed a good cavity – and these were now bearing fruit, particularly with the heavier engines and coaches.

In addition, the only method of signalling was by telephone, and nature saw to it that the poles, cables and junctions were quickly overgrown. We augmented this whenever possible by snapping cables – a process that on an earlier occasion nearly cost me my life. I had taken a good look around when walking up-country and, seeing no Japanese, had taken a running kick at a field telephone unit on the side of the track. Fortunately I slipped on the ballast, missed my objective, and turned around to find a soldier with a fixed bayonet at my back. He had been hidden behind the tall Englishman who was following me. I mustered a major piece of insouciance; and compensated my failure by cutting through the cable with my heel-plate a little later.

One of the main hazards of life now became flies. These and bluebottles had been with us throughout the line-work but they were mainly a nuisance through trying to eat our rice, with the accompanying risk of infection, and in settling on our bodies to drink our sweat. This problem was further compounded on 26 October by the evacuation of all the impressed civilians from the adjoining area: all their flies immediately migrated to us, and the daylight hours were a total misery.

The addition of plague to our other tropical diseases was reported from most camps on the line. I never discovered whether this was an accurate diagnosis, and the matter was an academic one in view of the total lack of any means of controlling such an infection. The huts were infested with lice, flies, bugs, mosquitoes, and we had no soap and hot water even for personal hygiene, and the only protection we could devise was to turn the tents inside out and leave them in the hot sun for as long as possible. The huts, which were by far the worst infected, merely took their chance.

Out of self-interest the Japanese now decided that something must be done to control the fly population, although this seemed to be very much the same type of situation as the one faced by King Canute. We were now issued with unwanted meat from the Japanese cookhouse – mainly offal – and in the tropical heat this was soon stinking. Using fly-swats made from any available material we killed thousands in the course of an hour, and if nothing was pressing on the line we kept at it for several hours each day. The results had to be given to the Japanese at the end of each session.

The stinking mass of filth and necrosis that the meat became now put ideas into the heads of our barbarians. They would force someone to eat it, despite all protests that this would result in almost certain death. They re-inforced their authority with boot, butt and bayonet, and in most cases the victim was soon dead.

Even the most dedicated Christian found it difficult to forgive such organised murder, although it was recognised that we were dealing with the lowest form of animal life, the decerebrate peasant.

In the post-war years many ex-FEPOWs have been accused of having an obsession about flies, none more so than myself. Such a charge is usually laid by people who have had no experience of epidemic diseases in tropical countries, and their enormous toll in health and lives. If DDT had proved the remedy that it originally appeared to be, malaria might have accompanied smallpox into history, and many millions of people who have succumbed to that dreadful disease may now have been alive.

Certainly most of the most lethal diseases of Asia are fly-borne – malaria, sandfly fever, dengue, etc. – and while it is admitted that cholera is a water-borne infection only a fool would ignore an invasion by multiple millions of flies on the presence of exposed samples of human faeces, many of which were known to be infected by dysentery, cholera and other enteric diseases.

In the absence of any medical help or sanitation, the greatest protection against both disease and weather was a hat, and the greatest of these was the Australian bush-hat with its wide brim. During the five to six months of the monsoon one's mess-tin rapidly filled with rainwater, and because of the exigencies of both hunger and allocated time it was necessary to consume this floating mess immediately or starve. Trial and error soon demonstrated that a combination of hat and head allowed the rice to be eaten with a minimum of rain, as the water simply cascaded from the brim onto one's knees and feet.

Even greater protection was provided during the dry season when combat was joined between humans and flies as to which of the species got the major portion of the rice. It was a cardinal rule to cover both the mess-tin and spoon between mouthfuls – and, where this was breached, to dispose immediately of any rice on which a fly had settled.

When I was thought to be dying in Roberts Hospital in 1942 my original bush-hat was stolen; and when convalescence and discharge confounded that prognosis I was issued with the bush-hat of someone who had been less fortunate, and I retained it through many vicissitudes until my release three-and-a-half years later.

Without using too many platitudes I hope I have made plain the inestimable value of the life-support system we had evolved through our friends; and, where circumstances have allowed it, many of those friendships continue as warmly and with gratitude to the present. Collinson, Henson, Harrison, Huckerby and I continued to share the good and the bad, to support and encourage in times of depression, and to hope collectively for an end to this brutish and wretched existence.

On 12 November 1943 the numerous clouds that surrounded us had acquired a very bright silver lining: I met Lieutenant J.E. van Zanten of the Dutch army, and thus commenced a friendship that lasted until his untimely death in a car accident in Holland in December 1962. His widow remains one of our closest friends. He was one of the unlucky members of the Netherlands East Indies Forces whom the Japanese transferred to the Siam rail operations. His wife and other members of his family were civilian internees in Java.

I have never known a man who, whatever the odds, carried himself more confidently and had the much-needed virtue in those circumstances of conveying that confidence to others. When we were surrounded by sickness and death, when the work effort was intense and sadism its constant companion, through severe starvation and his own ill-health, and later through all the phases of bombing by Allied planes, it was Jan who emerged smiling and encouraging.

Because he was an officer he recognized that he worked far less frequently, far less laboriously, and had a much higher income than the other ranks in either the Dutch or British forces, and he devoted all those advantages to others.

New friendships brought new interests: families, hobbies, experiences in the pre-war days, books, plans for the future; and displaced the repetitive conversations that one tended to have with long-established friends.

We met as often as we could. Now that the railway was through we worked much shorter hours, had more rest days, and the food had improved throughout the line because of better supply facilities. As a result we both acquired new friends in each other's huts and the new interests that went with them.

I know that the secret of Jan's confidence and his treatment of those around him lay in his devout Christianity. However easy it may be to follow the tenets of the Christian faith in leisured peace and affluence, our experience under the Japanese had made it much more difficult to 'see God in cloud and hear Him in the wind.'

But nothing shattered Jan's confidence that 'all things work together for good to them that love God', and it was the foundation of his entire life.

Within the camps he never went anywhere without his biscuit tin, and this was usually full to the top with Prophet's Beard and paper. Although he was a heavy smoker, he always dispatched the tin around the entire hut, and more often than not it was returned empty. He never once complained or showed displeasure, and never used his generosity and natural kindness to court popularity or gratitude. If this should sound like *de mortuis nil nisi bonum* it must be said that there are many people alive today who would gladly underwrite my comments – and not all of them were his beneficiaries. A relative of Jan's who was critically ill with paralytic diphtheria owes his recovery to the devoted medical care by the Dutch doctors, and to the provision of extra food through Jan's generosity.

Many people benefitted in this way, not least myself, and we were all forced to assume that, in such austere times, it was his food and finances that were sacrificed on our behalf.

Because of their long experience in the Far East, the Dutch from Java and Sumatra knew the tricks of the trade where food and its cooking were concerned, and generously shared their knowledge with us; what wild foods could be culled from the jungle and what was inedible, how to grind rice into flour and thus make pastry – things that we had neither the time nor the opportunity to discover for ourselves. Jan and I made evening trips into the jungle to collect parslin, a tough plant of questionable food value but once we had washed the animal droppings off and boiled it, it filled the empty spaces and dispelled the pangs of hunger.

☆　　☆　　☆

The rat population had now grown to such proportions that $1 was offered for each one caught. The response was so enthusiastic that the price dropped to 25c after twenty-one days. Although I never took part in these forays I was able to declare an interest in getting rid of the rats as my sole handkerchief was eaten from under my 'pillow' by one of these monsters while I was asleep – my pillow throughout captivity being a mess-tin wrapped in a hessian sack. Even the mess-tin had a story: my original, of tin, issued in England, rusted through and only half could thus be used. One of my friends, knowing of the problem, discovered a Dutch aluminium mess-tin next to a man who had died of cholera. He brought it back to the camp, we boiled it, and it is still in my possession. Being circular it didn't make such a good pillow!

On 25 November 1943 I commenced with a temperature of 103 degrees, and the worst headache I have had before or since, and malaria was confirmed. I told Jan all I wanted was a mess-tin of tea with a lime squeezed into it. This was akin to asking for manure from a wooden horse, and was made as a statement, not as a request that might be capable of fulfilment. It was typical of him that ten minutes later he returned with the mission accomplished, and never throughout history was nectar so wonderful.

On 30 November, thanks to the generosity of the British Government via the Swiss Legation in Bangkok we received thirty-one cigarettes each and one or two men were lucky enough to be allocated a piece of soap. We shared whatever we got with our Dutch fellow-captives but there was always a strong feeling that we had involuntarily shared them with the Japs as well.

At least we hadn't had the experience of other camps where the Japanese had bayonetted all the gunnybags containing cigarettes, ensuring that as many as possible were destroyed in the process; and at a civilian internee camp in Sumatra, they had mixed Red Cross supplies of jam, marmalade, cigarettes, butter and toilet paper in one huge mess, thus ensuring that the starving and dying inhabitants obtained no benefit at all.

Of all the contingents that went up-country to Siam it is possible that none suffered more grievously than those who became known as H. & F. Forces. Their time in Siam covered a period of eight months and slightly more than 10,000 men were involved in toto. When they were brought down to Tamarkhan and Kanchanaburi in December 1943 almost 4,000 had died, and many more were soon to follow. On their onward journey to Singapore the train had repeatedly to be stopped to permit burial. In his excellent official history *Death Railway* Clifford Kinvig records that one man reported that he had suffered from beriberi, pellagra, dengue fever, malaria, dysentery, blackwater fever, jaundice, scabies, ringworm, tropical ulcers, tropical pemphigus and tinea. If he reached home he may have discovered, as many of us did, that he was suffering from strongyloides and hookworm; but add to the above list a few violent beatings and a rail accident or two and a fairly representative picture emerges of the rail camps.

One evening in November 1943 I was asked by a distressed Englishman to go to the line, which adjoined the Tomajo camp, to see if I could help any of the sick on a train on its way south. After twenty-two months as a POW, and twelve months of this in Siam, I felt fairly case-hardened to anything the Japanese and Koreans could produce. But nothing could have prepared me for this appalling experience. Truck after truck of sick, dying, and apparently dead POWs. As we opened the doors the faeces ran out, the stench was appalling, and all the flies and bluebottles in the Far East appeared to have gathered for the occasion. I spoke to one man who was sitting with arms round knees and hands clasped, and asked if he would like a drink of water. When he neither spoke nor acknowledged me I tapped him on the shoulder but gained no response. The tell-tale heartbeat that was so easily visible between the ribs in major wasting was not apparent and I still have no idea whether he was alive or dead. In a little while Hirohito's heroes took their victims from the Allied forces on their journey. Less than two years before, these had been young men full of the joy of life: by organised neglect they had been reduced to the detritus of an already-doomed project.

On 2 December our party of five who had held together for a year began to break up when John Collinson was evacuated south through sickness.

On 12 December we moved south (twenty-five miles), to Hindate and I made a note of the times as an illustration of Japanese efficiency: 0700 Reveille; 0930 on lineside; 1630 moved off; stop at Pran Kassie station for three hours; further south for one hour, stop for truck derailed; arrived Hindato 0030 on 13 December. We had one pint of rice throughout this period to 0800 on 13 December.

We slept on the ground under a tent roof, and as there were no walls we were bitterly cold. The loss of bug-ridden bamboo was compensated by an army of mosquitoes which attacked us throughout the night. As with most people, I was sick with undiagnosed fevers, malaria, diarrhoea, anaemia, and the common vertigo and visual disturbance caused by starvation. There were, throughout this time, many instances of severe skin eruption, usually covering the entire body and originally diagnosed as being due to scabies. However, these usually cleared when the diet improved, and they were diagnosed as due to inadequate diet, particularly salt, which was almost unknown throughout our captivity.

We were adept now at building attap huts, and when the necessary materials were forthcoming we built several, each of which accommodated about 200. Unfortunately the Japanese could afford only sufficient bamboo poles and attap to install a roof, so we slept on the ground still, and remained cold and mosquito-ridden. With the passing of time we were able to erect bamboo slats for beds, and with true generosity we followed the now-standard tradition of sharing our bed-bugs with the Japanese. It was a simple matter to transfer several hundred to the Japanese huts and leave nature to complete the task.

Our second Christmas in captivity was now approaching, and we were determined to celebrate as traditionally as possible. I became a member of an ad hoc choir on 21 December and we had five practices by kind permission of our hosts. On the first of these we thought we were doing quite nicely in a small empty hut when a Japanese soldier burst in – all four feet ten inches of him – and began to scream at us in paranoic rage, threatening to shoot and bayonet us all. As usual, higher authority had forgotten to tell the night guard of our plans. As we had no hymn books and no paper we had to rely on memory for our entire contribution but we acquitted ourselves well. We carolled all the huts on Christmas Eve, and gave a carol service with the Dutch choir at 1730 hours. I hope that God made allowances for the Dutch/Javanese/English rendition.

On the 25th our cooks really went to town:

Breakfast: Sweet milky rice porridge. Fried egg Wavell.
Tiffin: Fish kedgeree. Fried steak, gravy, peas, and roast and chipped potatoes. Beef pie.
Dinner: Nasi Goreng. Baked jam roll with white sauce. Coffee.

At 2100 hours our entertainers laid on a wonderful camp concert; and we received from the CO presents of one tical, twenty cigarettes, one piece of soap and eight toffees per man. *Carpe diem!*

On Boxing Day we made up for our gross hedonism by walking eight miles on jungle tracks and rebuilding part of the road that had collapsed, and the following day did an

120

eleven-mile stint.

In January 1944 the rice issue was cut by 10 per cent as were the very meagre issues of other food: pumpkin, dried potatoes and 'rubber' fish – so called because they were dried in the sun and were akin to chewing indiarubber. We saw this as a sign of Japanese parsimony but recognised that they might be beginning to feel the pinch of war. After all, they had many thousands of troops in a very small area, and were daily transporting large military formations to Burma. Needless to say, they weren't issued with the manure rice that was our daily lot.

On 21 January we went through a phase of what seemed to be temporary insanity. We were issued with fourteen cigarettes from the International Red Cross, but there were such small amounts of sugar, soap, jam and biscuits that they were raffled. The insanity lay in the acquisition of skipping ropes, Ludo, boxing gloves, chess sets, cards, mouth organs and metal violins. We never believed that the IRC had intended the money to be spent in this way, and saw it as a rather macabre joke by the Japanese. As almost everyone had repeated fever and diarrhoea we never saw the boxing gloves and skipping ropes again, but a Dutchman, who was the leader of an orchestra, gave a wonderful classical concert on the violin, and received rapturous appreciation.

We continued with wood-chopping fatigues, line maintenance and road repairs throughout this time but the more welcome work lay in the gardens which we had made within the camp. Water was no problem as we were fairly near the river, and life was much more leisurely as there were insufficient guards to supervise each working party.

Our Japanese commandant at this time was a pathetically senile old man who had long outlived his capacity to fulfil any sphere in life usefully. Major Chida was reputed to have been in the army when the Japanese were still fighting with swords.

His treasured possession in this camp and the recipient of whatever warmth lay in his heart was a cow, from whom he was determined to extract a large quota of milk. Despite daily visits and soft words from him, and the supply of whatever fresh greens we had grown in the garden it adamantly refused to lactate. It was provided with rice-bags in its attap byre to insulate it from the cold ground and keep its udder warm and clean; still no milk!

Of course, the POWs saw in all this a kindred spirit that felt the same contempt for the Japanese as we did, and fearlessly expressed it.

Eventually, Chida realised that he was up against a superior force and as a punishment ordered that the rice-bags be withdrawn and the cow freed from the byre.

I am happy to record that on the day Chida and we left the camp the cow yielded its first consignment of milk.

On 11 March 1944 we were moved to what is now regarded by most FEPOWs as the parent camp in Siam – Non Pladuk – and we were in the No. 2 area. This was tented accommodation, and for the first time since Wam Po the latrines had attap roofs and walls, a degree of civilisation that saved one performing one's functions in full view of the camp. Although the river was far away we had ample water for washing, a great advantage in view of the frequent dust-storms that swept the area and the high weather temperatures during the day.

Here we had the best canteen of our experience, as we were near supplies and the Japanese were happy to let two men supervise it. If memory is correct they were Twist and Frost and I knew them both very well but we never saw any evidence that they lived up to the implications of their names. We had peanut toffee, tapioca flour cakes, small pies of questionable content, and anything that the camp's slender financial resources could afford on the odd occasions when purchase was permitted from the local population – duck eggs, dried whitebait, bananas, etc.

For the first time we were compelled to have shaven heads, a rule applying to all Japanese forces. This was a mixed blessing as the high temperatures and the blazing sun badly affected all those who had had a good thatch but no hat; it lessened the chances of getting head-lice, and allowed skin eruptions caused by our deficient diet to be kept clean. Even though our work-load had lessened and our food improved there were still diarrhoea, fevers, tropical ulcers, peripheral neuritis; and on the 20 March 1944 I noted in my diary that 'people now seem to offer no

GFK '46   LUXURY ATAP-HUT.   NON—PLADUK (No 2)

resistance (physical or mental) and just fade out – mainly malaria and dysentery.' To add to any tendency towards hypochondria the Japanese now forbade all church services, concerts or discussion groups: no reason was given for this but later analysis suggested that such proscriptions were frequently precipitated by set-backs to the Japanese war effort. At that time we had about 8,000 men in the Non Pladuk Nos. 1 and 2 camps and 2,000 were severely sick.

On 18 March 1944 I was re-admitted to our euphemistic hospital – this time with beriberi, malaria and internal bleeding of unspecified origin – this last had been almost continuous for nearly six months – persistent diarrhoea and bronchitis. There were occasional small doses of quinine but otherwise it was a case of keeping us out of the way of the more violent of the Japanese and Koreans, and waiting for the gross fluid-retention caused by the beriberi to disperse. As the Japanese reduced our rice ration by twenty per cent on three occasions in as many months the chances of overcoming any form of beriberi were slim, and by mid-August I had added increasing deafness and worsening of my eye trouble to the diagnoses already mentioned. However, I had to admit that I was in much better health than many of the others. Those of us with wet beriberi found little sympathy: because of the extra weight we looked well even though we could only walk with feet widely apart. Those with dry beriberi were grossly emaciated, every bone could be counted and they frequently walked with a staggering, high-stepping gait, and often fell. They were little more than ambulant cadavers, and this was emphasised by their wild, staring eyes and retracted upper lips.

On 5 September I was transferred to No. 1 area of Non Pladuk along with all the other hospital and convalescent sick, the MOs and orderlies; and on the following day several of the rest of No. 2 camp followed, including most of my friends.

Because it was immediately adjacent to the Bangkok/Singapore/Burma railway-line Non Pladuk was ideally situated to be a base and transit camp. In addition, on either side of the four or five lines that ran past the camp there was the Hashimoto marshalling yard; on the second side of the triangle that formed the camp there was a railway lay-by for laden trains with all the materials of war; and on the base of the triangle was Godayama's engineering works and an oil depot for the trains. Adjacent to the oil depot was a Japanese barracks. Inside the POW camp at the angle where Hashimoto and Godayama were separated only by the railway lines was an AA gun – a nice tight little collection of targets for the Allied Bomber Command.

We had heard the pukka-dink (absolutely true) news on 7 June 1944 that the allies had landed in France on the previous day; this had come by 'dicky-bird', as the forbidden camp wirelesses were known. At about the same time we heard disturbing rumours that London had been evacuated because of the death and destruction caused by a new bomb – a story that snowballed because of the doodle-bug, I suppose.

For some time now we had been aware of increased air activity, and the reaction by the Japanese and Koreans suggested that the source was not Japanese. There was a great deal of excited jabbering, bugles blew warnings, vehicles were dispersed, fires dowsed at night-time, and the gun was manned.

At 0215 hours on 7 September 1944 we were awakened by the sound of approaching planes flying very low, and within minutes we were undergoing intense bombardment of the camp and the surrounding area. This is exactly what we had anticipated with such fearful hope. The Japanese had refused to allow either trenches or an escape into the trees beyond the camp boundary. As a result, ninety-two died and several hundred were injured. Those who had had experience of aerial bombardment simply lay down on the ground; those who had not, ran, and were cut down in swathes by anti-personnel bombs. We spent a very unpleasant time stuffing bits of our dead friends into rice bags and laying them out in the camp area for the reconnaissance planes to photo on the same day at 1000 hours. After the war there was an unconfirmed rumour that the Japanese had 'let it be known' that Non Pladuk was a transit camp for Japanese troops.

When the inevitable happened they could always claim that the allies had killed thousands of their own troops. At least we took comfort from this evidence that things were now on the move to release us but how tragic that people who had fought so hard to survive the railway should now die through Allied bombs.

Although the hospital and convalescent huts were still fully occupied, the light sick had continued to work each day in the marshalling yards and engineering area, and as both had suffered severe damage we were now engaged on sorting the whole from the broken, and dumping the latter. As a result of continuous pressure the Japanese now allowed us to dig slit trenches against the inevitable repetition of the bombings.

We would have been greatly encouraged if we had known the Allies' new strategy with regard to the overall campaign: bomb everything that moves, or provides the means of movement. Thus roads, rails, rivers, bridges, marshalling yards, trains, troop transports, ferries, were subjected to systematic bombing, and we saw the results of this after the war in many places. However, such a policy caused grievous losses among the FEPOWs on the move, and in the POW camps, for the remainder of the war.

On 22 September I was finally discharged from the convalescent ward and continued to dig trenches. Much of this work was rendered useless by the terminal phase of the monsoon: walls of earth were washed down into the trenches, which quickly filled and became a quagmire, and no means existed for draining them.

On the 29 October at 0215 hours the bombers returned, with Non Pladuk obviously the principal target. We could see the planes very clearly in the moonlight and this time they dropped high explosive. The nearest bombs hit the lines about fifty yards away and shortly afterwards an enormous piece of dried earth came down vertically hitting me on the left shoulder and knocking me into the bottom of the trench. On completion of the raid I went to the medical hut, as the arm was useless and the shoulder severely swollen. It was thought by the MO that no bones were broken, and a sling was applied.

Fortunately the limbless, both from up-country and those resulting from the last raid, had already been moved to Na Kompaton, and only five of us were injured, all from debris from outside the camp, as no bombs landed within the

126

perimeter. Evidently the message conveyed by the ninety-two rice bags on the last occasion had been correctly interpreted, it being recognized that the Japanese would never treat their dead in this way.

In early November I received a small batch of letters from home and was greatly heartened by them, but it must be remembered that all such correspondence was almost a year old – and sometimes much more – and simply stated the position at the time of writing. As has already been said, the Japanese interpreters got their pay by false pretences: command directives were frequently incomprehensible, and the spoken messages might just as well have been in Swahili.

This failure to communicate was never better illustrated than in the case of a letter received by one of our own men. This contained the message, 'Never mind, son, don't let the Japanese bastards get you down', from which the interpreter had deleted the word 'Japanese', and inserted 'Nipponese', a nomenclature by which they prefer to be known. The remainder of the message was allowed to stand.

On the 28 November 1944, the Japanese insisted that we should hand over to them 'for safe keeping' all our valuables. Knowing the Japanese record of dishonesty in stealing our Red Cross supplies, and lying about up-country accommodation and conditions, we protested most strongly but to no avail. At least we extracted itemised receipts from them, but we regarded these as a waste of paper. So I said goodbye to the gold watch given to me by my fiancée, the silver pencil and cigarette case given by Lee Choon Eng as Singapore collapsed, and resolutely refused to hand over my gold engagement ring – one reason being that my hands were so swollen with beriberi that the ring was embedded in the flesh.

I have endearing memories of two birds at this time – one a reality and one a phantom. The former was a mynah of gifted intelligence and vocabulary who turned up on parade each evening, and drove the Japanese into manic fury by sitting on the head of one of the men in the very company that was being checked. When the Japanese struck out with their teak sticks, the bird flew up two feet, the stick passed between the bird's feet and the man's head, and the two then came together again. The loss of face that this caused was further exacerbated by our delighted laughter, and the repetition of this as the bird advanced to each company in turn. Despite every stratagem the bird was still functioning when I left the camp, and thoroughly enjoying itself.

The phantom was the product of a gunner who was able to produce a perfect onomatopoeia of a cock in full crow. As the Japanese forbade any such possession, the guards were meticulous in ensuring that working parties brought back no such treasures from outside the camp. Thus a loud cockcrow late at night or at early dawn would send every Japanese guard on a detailed search of all the huts while we simulated sleep and suppressed our mirth. On one occasion they actually fixed bayonets but I never discovered whether this was intended for the cock or its owner.

With the decrease in the amount of heavy labour, and the relative improvement in our food compared with the starvation on the line, we grew bolder at this camp. The Japanese had always, at odd intervals, held a ceremony when they faced Japan, spoke a series of phrases and responses, bowed, and then finished with an affirmatory 'Ush', – the equivalent of our Amen, I suppose. These ceremonies were always of tedious duration, and we were kept on parade throughout. So we turned to the east and repeated their orisons in gobbledegook. This always produced the anticipated beatings. However, the worst of these occurred when Major Chida, an advanced geriatric, was riding painfully along on a bicycle to our rear. He was so fascinated by all that he saw that he disappeared into the monsoon ditch alongside the road. Oh dear! How great was the retribution.

It was quite obvious by now that aerial activity was increasing each week, and that this was predominantly Allied. The sweeps by the Japanese fighters that had been so conspicuous during the campaign were no longer seen, and the odd Japanese bomber invariably flew low and sounded as though it was about to expire. All this was welcome evidence that we were gaining the upper hand, and we continued to yell encouragement whenever the planes came over – more to discomfit the Japanese than to advance our own cause, of course.

On 29 November Tamarkhan camp, to our north, was

heavily bombed and it was reported that casualties were high. We had always known that this was a prime target because of proximity to the two bridges over the river Mae Khlong, the metal and concrete one being the major bridge of the entire line. The wooden bridge that we had used in the initial stages of construction was now virtually useless, thanks largely to the enormous volume of water during each monsoon, and the debris carried on its surface. This frequently assumed the properties of a battering ram.

On 3 December I was detailed to go to that very area, and left behind at Non Pladuk all my friends. The reports on the bombing of Tamarkhan proved to be perfectly true, and several of my Signals friends had been either killed or injured, one having been buried alive for twenty minutes and then resuscitated. We were back to the old conditions experienced on the line: poor food in limited quantities, no medical help, and a strenuous work-schedule. We spent part of each day waist or neck deep in the filthy waters of the Mae Khlong, which was little more than a sewer for eastern Siam. We were able to free the accumulated flotsam of the last two to three years around the wooden bridge but the main structure was a major problem. The attempt to replace rotting or missing beams proved futile and in a few days the project was abandoned. The daily immersion caused many people to go down with bronchitis, malarial rigors increased, and the diarrhoea that had haunted everyone on the line-laying now returned.

As did the Allied bombers. On 3 December, twenty one planes flew over the area and bombed Non Pladuk fairly severely, with the inevitable deaths and injuries. On 13 December the immediate environs of our camp were bombed and I have a vivid memory of many B29 bombers coming in low and blanket-bombing the bridges, the AA gun and the rest of the riverside. I can still recall the 'branding-iron' on the nape of my neck at the thought of so many bombs in such a tiny area – and every one of them appeared to be coming at our shallow trenches.

On 17 December the adjoining Kanchanaburi camp was laid waste by aerial bombardment, and the hill above our camp was the northern turning-point for the planes. We could see them clearly, as full moon was approaching, and the noise was shattering. Our only casualty was caused by a Japanese machine-gunner, sited on the said hill, who fired into our camp, and took the shoulder off one of our men. He died very shortly after. On 24 December we had yet another visit but the planes flew on to another target.

On Christmas Day we had church services at 0815 and 0915, and the pantomime *Aladdin* at 1015 hours. Widow Twankey was brilliant and would have graced any London pantomime. A young Dutchman with a slim figure took the part of one of the court maidens, and had dressed in camp-made padded bra, figure-fitting pants, and a waist-to-ankle divided skirt made from the gauze part of a mosquito-net. He looked the part of a young and attractive female, both in dress and deportment, and when he brought cigarettes to the hospital after the show it was a study in psychology to see the number of men who pressed him to sit beside them, and all those who made any excuse to touch him, although all knew him to be a man. Remember that we hadn't seen a white woman for almost three years, and most of the Siamese women away from the town tended to be edentulous, their mouths and gums stained by years of licking betel nut. It is worth noting that despite bombs, disease and hard labour, the people in the camp before our arrival had spent many weeks in preparing the libretto, learning their parts and completing the scenery and other props.

The fare for our third Christmas in captivity was:

Breakfast: Rice with jam, scrambled eggs and rice-bread. Sweet coffee.

Tiffin: Small steak, fried pumpkin, roast potatoes; Christmas Pudding (of questionable content).

Dinner: Meat, pumpkin and sweet potato, rice; sponge cake; burnt rice coffee (no sugar).

Our month in Tamarkhan was noteworthy for two things: it involved the welcome cool season between the end of the monsoons and the start of the torrid, humid season which, from March to the end of May, heralded the return of the monsoons; and it saw daily evidence of the welcome increase in Allied air activity, not only in our camp and its

130

environs but in the wider sphere of what was obviously Malaya, Singapore, and seaborne targets.

However welcome such activity might be as a harbinger of our eventual freedom, it was recognized, of course, that many of our own people would fall victim to it, not only in the prison-camps but on the hell-ships in which the Japanese were transporting their captives to the tin and copper mines of Japan and to work on war projects from which they should have been excluded. Many of those ships were sunk en route with appalling loss of life but all of them were floating latrines with their occupants battened down throughout each day in tropical heat, without adequate food and water, and with faeces, urine and vomit cascading from bunks onto those below. Those who commenced the journey without dysentery, tuberculosis, diphtheria and beriberi frequently fell victim to them and the death-rate was frighteningly high. All the ships were the worn-out remains of the Japanese merchant navy, their engines exhausted by lack of maintenance and spares, and their ventilation systems totally unable to cope with the demands of several hundred grossly-sick people.

We had already had abundant evidence of the increased air activity throughout the line, of course, and in the middle of December we had a gruesome reminder of the sacrifice that now had to be made in the pursuit of freedom. Because we were only a small working-party we had had abundant room in the present camp. At 0300 hours we were awakened and told to double up as a large contingent had arrived by rail from the north.

Hardened as we were after almost three years to the innate cruelty of the Japanese, we were appalled by this latest evidence. Into the camp on improvised stretchers were brought several dozen FEPOWs, most of them severely injured in a bombing raid that had occurred during the previous week a few miles to the north. For eight days their train had lain in sidings while sparse military traffic had gone through. They had had virtually no food and water, and no medical attention. Their wounds contained either the bomb fragments or bullets of the raid and were massively putrescent with maggots and flies filling their every cavity and the stench of necrosis everywhere. The

131

death-rate that had commenced with the original raid continued throughout their short stay, and very few were left to continue their journey to the southern camps where food and water and medical facilities were available.

It was recognized that this was something more than the gross inefficiency of the Japanese – a symbol of their readiness at all times to inflict suffering and death on their hapless victims.

There can be few people who survived the total Siam experience who did not at some time come under the benign and protective influence of Lieutenant Colonel Phil Toosey, later Brigadier Sir Philip Toosey. He epitomised to all of us what was meant by an officer and a gentleman, courageous both in battle and the much worse dangers of the POW camps. His greatest claim to fame lay in his command of Tamarkhan during the building of the Mae Khlong Bridge when he was the much-beaten buffer between a particularly harsh Japanese soldiery and the many diseased and exhausted slaves in that infamous camp. Wherever he went he was the colonel – in much-patched shirt and shorts, pipe-clayed webbing-belt and anklets, and gleaming boots. In all his camps he was loved for the protection he extended to the officers and men he commanded – often to his own considerable suffering – and for the example of courage and confidence that he showed at all times – a vital contribution when death, exhaustion and collapsing morale were always in evidence.

During the many POW reunions held in London, Blackpool and Edinburgh he always gave the impression that he had come there to see *you* – and every person he greeted felt that – and I am honoured and grateful for his friendship over the many years, and for several delightful meals with his wife and him in Liverpool, London, Edinburgh, etc.

On 1 January 1945, we gave up all pretence of repairing the wooden bridge. We paraded at 1700 hours, and with typical Japanese efficiency we reached Non Pladuk at 0500 hours on the following day, a distance of approximately thirty miles! However, the day brought several rewards. I rejoined my friends Collinson, Van Zanten and Henson; and I received eighteen letters of widely-varying dates from home. The recipients of letters always received a tremendous lift to their spirits, and the news was always shared with one's closest friends. It provided material for discussion for many days. Not all the correspondence contained good news of course: the inevitable deaths in air raids, the wives who had run away, children who had died – some of whom had never seen their fathers: all these were calamities of enormous proportions to people whose response was limited by incarceration. We even had one young man who went around the camp telling everyone that he had become a father. When our suspicious minds asked the date of the birth of his son, we calculated that there was a gap of some two-and-a-half years between the possible date of conception and the birth. We left him in ignorance of the facts of life rather than raise doubts as to his wife's virtue.

On 15 January we were given one cotton handkerchief, one ounce of powdered tooth-cleaner, and one toothbrush. The last was particularly welcome as the brush taken into captivity three years before was suffering from severe alopecia. However dire the circumstances most of us had made a point of shaving whenever possible, even though soap and hot water were rarely available. Thanks to John Collinson's generosity we had shared his Rolls razor throughout our association, but the sole safety blade that I had was given in Roberts Hospital in April 1942, and was now becoming an instrument of torture, despite sharpening it on a Fuller's Earth jar whenever the possibility presented itself.

Hygiene in any form was rather an arcane concept, and what we had so easily taken for granted in freedom was now almost totally unobtainable. How we longed for a hot bath, an experience that had been in limbo now for over three years; regular dental hygiene; sharp scissors for our nails; the opportunity to wash with soap and hot water several times a day – and to dry on a clean towel. Proper dental examination instead of the rather makeshift stop-gap that our harrassed dentists were able to provide. Many of us who wore spectacles would have welcomed an eye test as poor nutrition had played havoc with our sight; and many of those who had lost spectacles through accident or bombing were severely handicapped.

Ringworm now appeared. It had always been in the camps, and one fellow was covered, literally from head to toe, with no hope of treatment, but it had never been a significant problem for most of us. We now slept in such close proximity on our split bamboo beds that contact was inevitable at some part of the night. When I discovered two rings on the inner surface of my left elbow and on the rear surface of my left thigh, I felt they called for immediate action before they spread. As bamboo is widely used as knives in the Far East, I made a chisel about a quarter-of-an-inch wide, a solution of Conde's fluid from crystals that I had carried since Changi, and burnt out the 'worm' by cutting away all the flesh in the area. Painful but completely effective.

Mental health ran a course from loss of memory to advanced psychotic conditions, caused by our way of life over several years without any relief; and the prospect of an untimely end at liberation, either through bombing and shelling by the Allied Forced, or through a policy of extermination by the Japanese.

I was worried to find that I could no longer place the furniture or pictures in the home I had lived in for twenty-five years. This experience was common to most people. As a mental exercise we would try to recall those things we had learned at school by rote – poems, songs, prayers, Latin declensions, etc. – and realised that we would come out bottom of the class. When working in pairs we would try to stimulate memory and powers of recall by one person stating five or six historical facts and then asking his partner to repeat them after a short lapse of time. At least it added interest to the tedium of the occasion.

Mention has already been made of the plethora of rumours in a POW situation. Some of them were meant to be a distraction, and made in good faith; some were purely idle and belonged to the field of mythopoeia; and some were meant to be a blind to disguise the news emanating from our concealed radio. So many of them were attributed to a smartly-dressed English-speaking Thai that we dismissed them when that was given as a source.

On 7 June 1944 I heard that France had been invaded on the previous day. We also knew by dicky-bird that the Duke of Kent had been killed in an air-crash in Scotland. We almost had brainstorms in trying to work out how the Russians were in Greece, only to find that it was a transmogrification of the 'rations being increased'; that the Queen Mary was sinking fast proved incorrect as both HM and the liner survived the war; and how on earth did we achieve a new Prince of Wales in early 1944? Certainly the battleship wasn't re-built! Churchill, Stalin, Hirohito, Tojo and Roosevelt had more peace talks than there were armies advancing down Burma in 1942, 1943 and 1944.

How accurate is the statement that the first casualty of war is Truth!

☆　　☆　　☆

Throughout our sojourn in Siam we had all been aware that, with better food and health and less forced labour, we could have had a wonderful experience.

As with most mountainous areas, whatever the associated climate, the views were magnificent once one was outside the tree barriers. There were vast panoramas of river, waterfalls, jungle and plain; brightly-coloured birds swept and called along the reaches of all the rivers, and wild orchids of every hue nestled in the crotches of many trees. Tropical countries always provide wonderful skyscapes with their towering thunderheads that so often warn of approaching storms, and these were complemented by the rising and setting of both the sun and moon in presentations that made both appear much larger than in the more northerly latitudes. We even, on one occasion, saw the proverbial blue moon. If we rose, as we often did, in the predawn, we saw the wreaths of the night mists disperse, watched the chaplets of mist around the pinnacles of rock slowly dissolve, and heard the piteous and heart-breaking cries of the gibbons as the sun rose.

When circumstances permitted we watched the many wild creatures with fascination: stick insects that assumed the pattern of the surrounding growth, camouflage that guaranteed instant invisibility; praying mantises that remained in permanent genuflection while seeking food; chameleons whose bulbous eyes in independent function

135

sought the food that their darting tongues so easily retrieved; and always, ubiquitously in home and factory, office and tree, that delightful little lizard, the gecko, chattering away while he chased his food.

Not all of them charmed us, of course. We hated the leeches who, unfelt and usually unseen, gorged themselves on our blood like mini-Draculas and then, replete, dropped off to digest their meal in comfort. We could force them off with a cigarette or ember but these were too rare to be of use in deep jungle. Pulling them off risked a tropical ulcer. We never discovered how they managed to cultivate their young between our toes but it was common to find minor colonies of them in those areas. These were more easily removed.

The poisonous creatures we frequently killed because of the threat they posed to near-naked people in crowded conditions, and the absence of any antidote; tarantulas (who usually evaded us at lightning speed), scorpions, snakes, millipedes and centipedes all constituted major threats to welfare, although hunger made us bold towards the end and we killed the snakes for food.

Throughout the world there are many varieties of ant, and Siam was host to several of these. Disturbed, those industrious creatues formed a formidable army and many of us were severely bitten when we disturbed the tropical growth. The bugs in our Jap-happies (G strings) provided a rich source of food for them, and we whiled away many a boring parade by flicking bugs on to the ground. Being lucifugous they fled for the nearest cover, usually hotly pursued by the ants, who turned them on their backs and cut off their legs while they enlarged the entrances to their homes. Incidentally, it was always a miracle to us that the bug could convert human blood to anything so foul-smelling as its crushed body demonstrated, and the ant was welcome to the meal. I know nothing that smells worse in the whole gamut of nature, dead or alive.

There was yet another creature to torment us, and this was principally in our leisure hours. Whenever we bathed or washed our blankets or rice-bags in the river we were severely bitten by groups of sabre-toothed fish. We never managed to catch one as they moved so quickly, but their

P.o.W. CAMP. SIAM. (NON-PLADUK No.2) G.F.KERSHAW 1946.

bite was painful, even though I never recall their removing any flesh.

☆   ☆   ☆

On 17 January 1945, without any regrets, we moved from Non Pladuk to Na Kompaton. The former had been severely damaged by bombs, many people had been killed and injured, and the shell of the engine and waggons, now welded to the rails on the northern perimeter, was symbolic of all that we had undergone there. The blaze caused by the 5000 gallons of high-octane fuel ignited in one of the raids had given us all a great deal of pleasure and was seen as one more contribution to the defeat of the Japanese.

Our new camp was conspicuous for many things, all of them good. Our standard of living was probably higher there than at any other time in captivity, the food and accommodation improved, the canteen had a much better stock of food, and we were immune from bombing, at least during the three months that I was there. This last may have been due in some part to the enormous gold-covered Buddhist temple that adjoined the camp which, while it may have provided a marker for aerial navigation, certainly indicated the presence of our hospital camp.

By all pre- and post-war standards for hospitals this one was a travesty but for the first time we had the means to deal with serious illness, the many thousands of tropical ulcers with their oft-associated amputations, and the results of rail accidents and bombings. The huts were built of bamboo and attap with their customary distribution of dust and bamboo lice and bugs, and the operating tables and chairs were of bamboo. Sterilisation of instruments was by the use of the petrol tin with boiling water, but at last the Japanese had been persuaded to supply a meagre amount of drugs, dressings and surgical instruments. (Until now the only bandages we had seen had done duty as laces on the football boots of opposing Japanese and Korean teams); surgical saws and scalpels replaced the razor blades and wood saws that had done duty in the primitive up-country camps. Clifford Kinvig in his excellent book *Death Railway* records that at one time there were 8000 patients and in the

138

nineteen months it functioned 1000 operations were performed by a team of Australian, British, Dutch and American surgeons. Of the 10,000 patients brought to the hospital in that period the mortality rate was only 2.8 per cent – remarkably low, as Kinvig says, in view of the primitive conditions and lack of proper medical supplies. It is worth noting that the American Red Cross supplied many of the medical materials in May 1944.

Minor miracles were performed in the amputees' post-operative phase by the provision of artificial limbs. In civilian life, loss of a limb may be a shattering experience when related to bread-winning, walking, sport, motoring and so on. In those conditions it could be lethal, particularly when associated with beriberi, peripheral neuritis and vertigo.

The only materials available for such prosthetics were kit-bags, valises and side-packs, all of which were now several years old and had undergone major trauma in many transits and monsoons. A tailored socket to take the stump, straps to attach it to the wearer's waist, and a wooden or bamboo leg did as much for the morale of the patient as the knowledge that he had lost a limb whose septicaemia threatened his life.

Throughout our up-country experience a combination of malnutrition, hard labour, and bare legs and feet, had caused a high turnover of those dreadful ulcers. In twenty-four to thirty-six hours a small injury to the surface of the skin could become an ulcer covering the whole of the shin with wide lateral distribution. The absence of dressings and antiseptics and the invasion of the wound by thousands of flies soon resulted in acute septicaemia. Heroic efforts were made – both by surgeon and patient – to remove the sepsis by scraping the entire wound with a sharpened spoon, while the patient was held down by his companions; but the screams and the results of this primitive surgery were so appalling that amputation was usually the last resort. In many cases death made the most merciful decision, where the chances of any medical approach were non-existent.

The 300 men in my party went not as patients but as workers, in order to build a defensive bund and ditch aound the camp, and we saw this as one of the most encouraging

139

signs to date. After all, the Japanese would hardly be excluding possible invaders or more tightly incarcerating their captives if the Japanese forces were occupying India, Burma and points north. The dimensions of the ditch escape me but probably it was two metres deep by two-and-a-half metres wide and the displaced soil became the outer wall of the camp. Thus on the inside of the camp the wall and ditch combined totalled four metres, – a formidable barrier to any attempt at escape; combined with the ditch, a severe hazard to any invader. On Japanese instructions – against all the articles of war – we built four pill-boxes, one in each corner. However, instead of building them one to each side we built them in two pairs facing each other, thus ensuring that the Japanese fired directly at each other. In addition we built the apertures to suit our height and not theirs. Despite frequent inspections by senior Japanese officers, these two hazards were never noted, and were there when we left the camp.

The use of the temple as a navigation point by the RAF and the USAAF provided me with an opportunity to give a great deal of pleasure to several of my friends and a good deal of misery to a Japanese soldier. The Japanese always referred to the huge B29 bombers as B29 San (Mr B29). As we broke off for 'lunch' one day I spotted one on a direct approach to the camp. Immediately ahead of me there strutted a very self-important Japanese soldier whom I tapped on the shoulder and indicated the approaching plane. Without hesitation he jumped head-first into the ditch and the several inches of glutinous mud in the bottom. The indignity and loss of face that he suffered were now compounded by the necessity of having to ask several of his captives to help him out as he was too short and slippery to climb out unaided.

Na Kompaton was a large camp with the so-called healthy personnel segregated from the sick. The bund and ditch were therefore a major project at which we worked for seven hours per day. The deeper we dug, of course, the higher we had to throw the soil to build the adjoining wall, and the entire surface had to be as smooth as a billiard table when completed. The top of the wall became a sentry-beat so that the Japanese on duty had oversight of the entire area, both inside and outside the camp. One large entrance provided access to the outside world, and we built suitable defences against attack at that point. Although we were kept hard at work there was little of the violence that had been experienced up-country, and those with dysentery, malarial rigors, and grossly-swollen limbs through beriberi were allowed to take life more easily.

For obvious reasons I never recorded in my diary the many incursions into our camps of the dreaded Kempetai, those moronic thugs who ranked alongside the Gestapo and the NKVD in their pursuit of torture, persecution and execution. Indeed, it is difficult to decide which of us were the more frightened of them – the other Japanese soldiery or ourselves. They had no respect for rank, and on more than one occasion we saw them go with a fine-tooth comb through the effects of senior officers on their way by troop-train to Burma. Such officers weren't allowed near their possessions, and walked around in patent anxiety and fear until the examination was over. It is hard to know what they were looking for on such occasions: they were entitled to exclude radios, with which we could communicate with our allies, weapons of any sort, and messages to and from the special operations people who, they must have known, were operating in the area. They descended on a camp at speed, usually when we were absent at work, spread into the huts and began their search before the sick-in-camp could take evasive action.

Diaries were forbidden, as were all writing materials, so the maintenance and preservation of personal diaries presented problems. Japanese guards walked through the huts at all times, and were only too happy to advance their own interests. The long working days and total absence of rest days while building the railway had meant that, in the absence of any artificial light, weeks passed when no writing could be done, so full advantage had to be taken as opportunity presented itself. Crowded huts and helpful friends provided the most security on such occasions, and it was a simple matter to cover the diary until the threat had passed.

As with all Japanese proscriptions, punishment depended on the Japanese involved, and there appeared to

141

be no code by which infringement could be judged. The oriental mind works in peculiar ways, and while one Japanese authority might see execution as the only answer to a crime, another might find a severe beating to be adequate punishment. The labile temperament of all Japanese meant that decisions were frequently made on mood – and the good or bad outcome was the result of that mood.

But with the Kempetai, tolerance and understanding of prevailing circumstances were unknown. They were professional thugs and murderers, and had only one justification for their barbaric existence: to find as many of their own army, the POWs, the civilian internees, and the civilians of the occupied countries as possible guilty of crime, and to inflict the maximum punishment. It is possible that the twin slogans 'The Greater East-Asia Coprosperity Sphere', and 'Asia for the Asiatics', were destroyed more by the 'Kempie' than by any other factor associated with the Japanese occupation of South East Asia.

Thus it was that Leonard Wilson, Bishop of Singapore, and his colleagues in Changi Gaol, were mercilessly tortured by beatings, by the water treatment that repeatedly takes a person to the point of death and then revives him, and by thirst and starvation so that many of them died; that four officers and a sergeant-major, caught elsewhere with a small wireless receiving set, were beaten for hours on end until two of them died and the remainder were sent to the obscenities of Outram Road Gaol, Singapore, for imprisonment. That Captain Drower and other officers were violently beaten and then made to stand in front of the guard room for three days. All but Drower were then released. He was placed in an uncovered hole in the ground which was partly filled with water. He was kept there for six-and-a-half weeks. For the first three days he received no food or water. After this treatment he received two rice balls and water twice a day to drink. He wasn't allowed to wash or shave. After seven weeks, when he was on the point of dying, the Japanese agreed that he should receive proper nourishment and he was placed in a Japanese detention cell behind the guard-room, and he remained there until the surrender of Japan three weeks later.

In *Ban Pong Express* J.H.H. Coombes writes, 'The Japanese ordered that all diaries be handed in for their perusal – if considered harmless they would be "chopped" and given back. Any person subsequently found in possession of a diary which had not previously been handed in would be subject to serious disciplinary action – death if necessary.'

So what to do? We knew from the early days in Singapore, when the Japanese ordered that all books be handed in for approval, that only a limited number would be returned: the Japanese had neither the interpreters nor the interest to vet them. We reasoned, therefore, that they were much more likely to destroy en bloc all those personal records of their atrocities in the up-country camps. In any case, cigarettes, fear and monsoon downpours had seen the end of many of the early efforts.

So we just sat tight and never submitted them. I was caught out on two occasions – the first when the camp Japanese had a flash search and turned up my two diaries. I anticipated confiscation and arrest, but after a perusal of several minutes they were thrown down and left. On the second occasion the Kempetai stormed the camp and entered each hut simultaneously.I was sick-in-camp with dysentery, and as the diaries were lying flat in the rice-bag my only hope was to sit on the bag, tent my blanket over my head and feign sickness. The atmospheric temperature plus the heat inside my 'tent' combined to leave my face a beautiful scarlet. When the Kempie approached me I made myself as blear-eyed as possible, said 'Takusan bioki – malaria', (very sick – malaria). This would normally have had little effect, but he examined the remainder of my kit and moved on.

Thereafter I was much more cautious. Attap roofs are built in layers, as are tiles in ordinary houses, and it was a simple matter to slip one's diaries between two layers and to leave them there between entries. All one had to do was to ensure that one remembered their exact site, and that they hadn't been blown or washed to the outside of the roof during storms. I gratefully record my indebtedness to John Collinson and others who 'cached' my diaries in times of emergency, and guarded them so carefully during my emergency admissions to hospital.

One of those admissions occurred at this time, and it is worth recording because of the monumental generosity that it involved. We worked non-stop from 19 January 1945 until 30 March, and on this latter date we were given our first day's break. Thanks to the exhausting digging of the bund, the deteriorating quality of the food, and frequent attacks of malaria most of us were in poor shape and even the Japanese realised that we couldn't continue. I was so bloated with wet beriberi that I could walk and bend only with the greatest difficulty, as the skin tension reached bursting point. (I knew several people whose legs burst spontaneously).

My British MO diagnosed that there were many worse cases than me and he could do nothing for me. This so concerned a Dutch MO that he admitted me to his unit immediately, mainly to take me away from the heavy work. I was advised to get as much nourishment as possible but as I had no money and refused to sell my only asset – my gold ring – I was unable to implement this. With his customary compassion John Collinson visited me daily, and eventually asked if I could arrange to sell a shirt for him via the daily camp movements of people. I cautioned against this as this was his last item of clothing, and we all felt that the war was due to last for several years yet. However, his arguments prevailed, and when the transaction was completed he insisted on giving me, unconditionally, more than half of it. From outside sources I was able to buy eggs, peanuts, bananas etc., and within two or three days I began to pass water at a truly alarming rate, almost non-stop – and had assumed normal dimensions in less than a week. Such generosity carried the gift of life, and was compassion of Samaritan proportions, particularly when the war appeared to be stretching beyond the dimensions of time.

In April 1945 I added yet another name to that list of enduring friendships on which my survival was based: Oscar Stinson. We continued the process of buttressing each other's spirits, frustrating boredom, sharing one's few goodies, planning post-war lives and meals – a vast psychotherapy that had had such beneficial effects throughout captivity. In our meetings since in both Africa and

144

England we laugh over the stratagems that defended and sustained sanity in those times but the older we get the more we see them as the foundation of our survival.

Although our camp remained secure from air attack there was abundant evidence of activity elsewhere, and of the failure of the Japanese to combat it, both of which features greatly encouraged us. The air-raid alarm – the sonorous intoning of the huge bell in the forecourt of the temple – sounded on many occasions but planes either failed to appear or passed harmlessly to other destinations.

On one occasion at about 1300 hours I had had my rice and was half-way through having my hair cut outside the hut when the whole world came apart. It was one of those occasions when the senses are unable to accommodate the immediate transition from peaceful sunshine to ear-shattering and mind-disorienting noise. We soon realised that several USAF fighter-bombers had passed over us at tree-top height and with wonderful accuracy had dropped their bombs on the mess-room and quarters of the adjoining Japanese camp – while the Japanese were having their meal. The entire target-area erupted in smoke and dust, and we subsequently heard that most of the occupants had been killed. On this occasion the Japanese paid dearly for siting a military area next to a POW camp: only a fence separated the two sites but it seemed probable that the layout of our camp provided the release-point for the bomb-aimers. We were entirely unscathed.

Around this time we heard further evidence of Allied activity. Late at night and into the early hours, without the sounding of the air raid warning or air activity, we heard a furious bombardment to the sout-east, and assumed this to involve Ratburi on the Gulf of Siam. We were able to confirm the accuracy of this assumption within the next few days.

On 11 April 1945 1000 of us were paraded at 0900 hours, searched in some detail, – without my diaries being discovered – and then allowed to return to our huts. The assurance from the Japanese that we were to be transferred to a new camp, with electricity, showers and good food aroused our worst forebodings, as such lies had always been the precursors of disease, death and squalor. We showed our scepticism and incredulity with several comments that didn't require a knowledge of the English language to be understood. We paraded again at 2330 hours on 11 April and at 0200 hours on 12 April left Nakompaton by train in a southerly direction for an unknown destination. We travelled thirty-five to an open truck, and, as we were now pulled by a wood-burning engine, our hair and skin were soon burnt by the particles of burning wood blown out of the smoke-stack. At 0900 we passed through a torrential rain-storm. We detrained at 1030 hours at Chulalongkorn Bridge, Ratburi, the area of the naval bombardment of the previous week. The shelling had been so accurate that the two central sections had collapsed at their adjoining ends into the water. The Japanese had connected these at near water-level with a wooden platform, thus forming a crude U with outward-sloping sides. Over this we now had to carry our kit, Japanese kit, rice Kwalis, rice stocks, etc., to a paddy field some eight kilometres further south. Because of the Allies' denial of all forms of transport belonging to the Japanese we now holed up until 2130 hours, and then continued south until 0600 hours on 13 April when we detrained at Prachuab Kirikhan on the east coast of Siam. With customary inefficiency our arrival was totally unexpected, and no rice was forthcoming until 0900 hours. Thus in thirty nine hours we had each had six small slices of bread, two onion rissoles and two hard-boiled eggs.

At 1500 hours on that same day we left Kirikhan and walked by narrow jungle tracks for twenty kilometres in bare feet, and carrying all the kit already mentioned plus a large assortment of changkals (large-blade hoes), shovels, pickaxes, tree axes, heavy-duty ropes, crow-bars, dynamite and hammers. Of the 1000 men on this assignment only 300 of us had worked through from the railway via the bund continuously. Many of the other 700 men had been inpatients of Nakompaton for some considerable time, and several had had surgery so they were in no fit state to carry such loads in such gruelling conditions. However tough one's general condition and feet, carrying all that weight over mountain passes of gravelly mud would have made even a sherpa quail; and where sheer cliffs disappeared into the gorges below, one slip could have meant hideous death.

Iron kwalis could only be carried on one's head, and, because they were so fragile, shattered when dropped: not only did this qualify for a severe beating but experience showed that this would have meant loss of rice-cooking facilities at one of the later camps. On the following day we marched twenty-one kilometres with the same burdens, after a night on the ground in a very shabby attap hut. We were less than encouraged to meet a large party of Chinese coolies going in the opposite direction. They told us that they had refused to work any longer for the Japanese because of the high sickness and death rates, and prophesied that we should all soon be dead. On the same day we were attacked by large colonies of leeches in the deep jungle, and as we had no fire we burnt them off with lighted cigarettes, and the smouldering rope that we now carried whenever possible. Our food was the usual rice, and one very small piece of dried fish at midday, and plain rice at night.

On the 16 April we marched the final fifteen kilometres and came to rest at a small clearing in the jungle, which had the remnants of attap huts and had obviously been the home of the Chinese we had passed on the previous day. It was littered with their debris and all the evidence of haphazard occupation. No attempt had been made to repair the roofs against the frequent tropical rainstorms, wood and bamboo beams harboured snakes and scorpions, and stagnant water bred the mosquito larvae that made the area highly malaria-prone. There was no evidence of latrines so we assumed that the Chinese had used the periphery of the camp for toilet purposes.

On that final day we had dropped off parties of 200 and 300 at each of two similar squalid areas, and what we now named Moaner's Creek was thus the highest camp on what was subsequently named the Mergui Road – six kilometres from the Burma border and en route to the town of that name on the west coast.

The effort of those four days was as bad as anything we had experienced on the line. We had commenced the march more like beasts of burden than humans but as time passed we collected the kit and tools of the men who had been in hospital until the previous week, many of whom were almost too weak to stagger along. They were suffering from the usual vertigo and loss of visual accommodation, and diarrhoea bothered most of us. The fitter among us now paired off, put two bamboo poles about twelve feet long on our shoulders, and on these the Japanese hung their kit, our sparse possessions, that of the sick men, ropes, rice stocks, and, for good measure, split the shovels and changkals among us. On the final day I carried seven shovels and six changkals on my shoulders, as well as the laden bamboo poles. However, on that march there was little of the violence that had been so common on the long up-country marches: people weren't kicked and beaten to death when they collapsed, nor were they abandoned to the jungle when they were too weak to walk. For once the Japanese realised that they had a contingent of 1000 expendable men, most of whom were already sick and suffering from beriberi, and if they were to have any hope of completing their allotted task they had to husband their resources. We would have benefitted from unlimited drinking water but we were now in high and dense jungle and such supplies were rarely available. We were back now to the line days when our mouths became so gummy and our tongues so swollen that we were unable to communicate sensibly.

At the commencement of this march there occurred another of those experiences that did so much to cheer us up and lift the cloud of depression that engulfed all of us on occasion. As we left Prachuab we strung out in Indian file and were immediately joined by a small dog of unknown pedigree, who walked right up the column, looking up to each face as though seeking a known friend, and then repeating this on the way back. Whomever he sought wasn't there, of course, but despite our efforts to get him to return to base he persisted in his escort duties to the topmost camp and became the cherished friend of all of us. As has already been remarked, most of the canines in the Far East are pi-dog – mangy, flea-bitten creatures with battle-scarred coats, and eyes and ears missing. Bend down and they rush away from the anticipated stone or piece of wood.

With blinding originality we named our new friend Jungle. He was young, healthy, in immaculate condition, and was obviously used to human contact and a great deal of love. We assumed that he came from the home of some axis or neutral person resident in Prachuab, but we feared for him at the hands of the Japanese, who had amply proved their wanton bestiality towards all creatures. His coat was tan and dark brown, with occasional white markings, and he walked with a bright eye, with his ears pricked and with a jaunty step.

We commenced work on the following day on what was largely a repetition of our previous experience, except that we were now building a road instead of a railway trace. The trees were so tall and grew so densely that we were able to see the sky only by looking immediately above us. Firstly we hacked and we blasted and we chopped until sufficient trees could be removed to enable a track to be dug; and because we were traversing mountain slopes we started on the higher side with changkols and shovels, and threw the soil and boulders across to the lower side, where it became part of the road. This became our daily and back-breaking stint, made no easier by torrential rain – which made the area a quagmire – appalling rations and the bitter cold of the jungle, particularly at night. We started each day with a pint of pap-rice, which our natural functions disposed of within half an hour – had more rice at 1300 hours, and our evening meal consisted of rice and very small portions of dried vegetable and dried fish.

These factors, combined with a workshift of fifteen hours per day (0700 hours to 2200 hours), ensured an early return of all the problems we had had in the north: beriberi, general and cerebral malaria, dysentery, lacerated feet, visual and aural problems and extreme emaciation.

On our return to camp from our first day's work we realised that one of our men had been badly injured as we followed a trail of blood for a large part of the way. We learnt that when felling a giant tree he had run in the wrong direction and had been almost totally scalped by a whipping branch. He was deeply unconscious and suffering from almost total anaemia. When it was indicated to the Japanese that he was unable to eat and would require feeding by tube they generously gave one egg for his life support! I never heard the outcome as he was sent down-country the following day.

Although we now had no idea of the general war situation, either in Europe or Asia, and our dicky-bird had been left behind, logic suggested that if we were building a road across the Kra Isthmus it could only be to aid the Japanese war strategy. If the railway we had built was functioning and the Japanese had not been denied the use of the Gulf of Siam and the Andaman Sea by the Allies why build a road through dense jungle subjected to monsoon rain and with no port at its termination? If only we had known of the Chindits, of Bill Slim, and the battles around the Salween and Irrawaddy, of Kohima and Imphal, I wonder how many more men would have survived that final catastrophe – and the reason for a Japanese bolthole would have been abundantly clear. Now it was their turn to retreat!

By 26 April, and continuing the work done by the Chinese whom we had replaced, we had cleared a continuous track through the jungle equal to the width of two lorries, and built the road and bridges. We were back to a speedo phase and frequently worked from 0900 hours until 0100 hours on the following day, the last few hours being always in total darkness because of the great height of the trees.

There is a common misconception by many people that Asia, India and Africa enjoy a constant heat-wave, and that it is almost impossible to be cold in those countries. Nothing could be further from the truth: with the constant and torrentially heavy rain of the monsoon it was almost impossible to keep warm, even when working hard, and any pause – either while waiting for supplies or having a yasume – soon produced chattering teeth, and, quite frequently, extremely painful colic.

When the first lorry went through on 26 April it was abundantly apparent that the road as it stood would be very little use for heavy traffic. So much rain had fallen that, even with our help, the lorry made slow progress in an axle-deep quagmire. We reverted to our railway practice of attempting to ballast at least one track with rock debris from the blasting, boulders, and branches from the felled trees. Fifteen hours of non-stop work only served to emphasize the futility of our efforts, and the uselessness of changkols, shovels and baskets to tackle such a problem.

On 28 April we were given a day's holiday, and a Red Cross issue of Thai tobacco, one tin of peanut butter for the camp, some dried milk and beans; and to mark the opening (but not completion) of the road the Japanese issued one fluid ounce of saki and a few peanuts per man.

Our 'accommodation' continually leaked in very many places, swarmed with flies, bugs and lice, and dysentery and beriberi were again on the increase. Although we had devoted doctors with us, with, by now, a vast experience of tropical diseases and the effects of prolonged starvation, their efforts rarely got beyond the diagnostic stage, as they were almost totally without the means to treat any condition. The news was equally depressing from the two lower camps, and whenever we were in touch while on working parties our main conversation was in seeking news of the survival of our friends in each other's camps.

The effect of these conditions was calamitous so far as Jungle was concerned. From being a sleek, well-groomed and jaunty dog his physical condition had deteriorated so much that I doubt if his owners would have recognized him. His transition from good food to manure rice had been as rapid as had ours, and we had no means of augmenting his diet. It was a point of honour with all of us to contribute to his meals from our meagre issue but it was quite apparent after the first month that he was going downhill, at least physically. Mentally he was even more robust than before, and he faced what appeared to be the first major challenge in his life with outstanding courage and determination. He made no secret of his hatred of the Japanese and growled quietly whenever they came near him, thus making himself a target of their brutality.

Because of the extremely cold and wet weather and the risk of snakes we encouraged him to sleep inside the hut, usually under the bed space. In the early days at Moaner's Creek we were packed cheek by jowl and it was impossible to take him onto the bed for our mutual comfort. However, as death diminished our numbers quite rapidly he took to sleeping on or immediately under the bed of one of his friends. In the early hours of one morning he woke me with his warning growl when he was sleeping against the straw-

151

matting 'wall' and under my bed space. I saw the Japanese guard pass down the hut and a few minutes later a fixed bayonet was thrust violently through that same straw wall, narrowly missing my head and leaving Jungle untouched. The soldier had seen it as an opportunity to while away the boredom of the night and to rid the world of a lovely animal.

However much we tried to protect Jungle we were defenceless against the bayonets and brutality of our captors. On one occasion they gave a length of rope to one of our company sergeant-majors and ordered him to capture Jungle and take him to them. Their intentions were obvious as they had built a roaring fire of bamboo. With total confidence in a friend, Jungle allowed himself to be caught and we watched with increasing horror as our friend was dragged towards an agonising death.

When he was almost within reach of the Japanese the CSM did a most dramatic slip. His hands went up and Jungle took the opportunity to disappear into the surrounding trees. Unfortunately, the CSM paid for his heroism with his life. The slip was seen as intentional – which it undoubtedly was – and he was so violently beaten up that he died on the following day from his injuries.

The Japanese continued to be relentless in their pursuit, and on a later occasion captured him in one of the large bamboo baskets in use all over the Far East. They are immensely tough and very sharp and made for prolonged use and hard work.

On this occasion the heroes of Hirohito's army dragged the basket along with their bayonets, rather than risk the teeth of the trapped Jungle. Knowing the toughness of these baskets it seemed to us onlookers impossible that he could free himself in the few remaining yards before yet another bamboo fire.

But he managed it. He tore aside sufficient cross-pieces of the woven basket to force his body through, and once again he made for the surrounding trees. He had learnt by now that he was as welcome in the other two camps as at Moaner's Creek, and thither he would repair for days at a time, returning only when the Japanese there made his life unbearable.

☆　　☆　　☆

The assumption that, with the road open, our lives would be easier proved as vain as it had done with the completion of the railway. We were able to assess the transport problems between Prachuab and ourselves when our bulk rations were delivered by elephants. It was apparent that the road was made impassible by the same sea of deep mud that existed in our immediate area. Half-track or full-track vehicles are the only ones able to negotiate such conditions, and the Japanese had only standard lorries whose spinning wheels served only to dig themselves deeper into the ground and thus enlarge the quagmire, which continued to deepen as the monsoons progressed.

The only commodity freely available to combat this was of course trees; and we were now ordered to fell the smaller ones and chop them into four-metre lengths. Teams with blunt axes felled and lopped the trees, and the remainder of the men carried them to the appropriate site and dropped them transversely – where they promptly disappeared below the surface. The Japanese would allow only one man per carried tree, and the combination of raw bark on bare shoulder, and the knee-deep mud and bare feet, proved equally as exhausting as anything we had known on the line. Soon our feet were competing with our shoulders for the larger area of raw flesh.

On 17 May 1945 two of us did a round trip of thirty kilometres (almost twenty miles) in our bare feet. On the outward journey of fifteen kilometres we carried a sack of what appeared to be nuts and bolts slung on a bamboo between us; and for the last three kilometres of the return journey a 220 pound bag of rice. Much of the return trip was done in total darkness as we didn't reach camp until midnight.

By the end of May, after six weeks of work on the Mergui Road, the effects of a starvation diet, almost constant rain, lack of sunshine and an almost total absence of drugs were producing a situation very similar to the worst days on the line. Thanks to the isolated nature of our camp we had no cholera but dysentery, malaria, typhus and beriberi were more prevalent than on any previous occasion. To these we now added Weill's Disease, whose source is always rat-borne. One of my friends from Egham contracted this, and because of his fiercely independent spirit, refused to allow his friends to help him to the latrine. He made his final effort on elbows and knees, and at the half-way point rolled over on his side, dead.

Even if the Japanese had had the food and the will to deliver it to us, the means to do so was now lacking. On the railway the line-layers had at least always had the advantage of train deliveries, even if the quantity and quality left a great deal to be desired. In our present circumstances we would have gladly accepted the boiled seaweed of previous issues: it at least gave the jaws some work to do and gave the feeling of a full stomach for some considerable time. All we had now were the smallest possible quantities of low-grade rice and dried vegetables of the most revolting taste. (At the end of hostilities the Japanese in the three Mergui camps admitted that they had kept the fresh vegetables and quinine for themselves, against orders).

On 25 May we moved lock, stock and barrel to Tagare camp fifteen miles down the road towards Prachuab. This was a riverside camp, and similarly derelict and leaking. It was so badly overcrowded that there was no hope of avoiding the cascade of water that came through most of the roof but we had been well trained to accept it as stoically as possible.

Even the Japanese recognised that the road was useless with a wood foundation, and bullock carts were brought up to allow rocks and gravel to be filled into the worst areas. It is probably superfluous to say that we were the bullocks, and the effort required to transport these brakeless vehicles over steep mountain tracks covered in mud was almost superhuman. We were too weak to run with them when they ran away downhill, and the uphill work was equally exacting.

On one of these trips, cries were heard coming from the jungle, and were traced to one of the men who had 'gone missing' two or three days before. He had been without food and water in the interim, but the most distressing feature of his general condition was that he was covered in leeches. Like all of us he was virtually naked, and these disgusting things, bloated with his blood, were in every crevice of his body and all over his skin. Dehydration, starvation, leeches, and the conviction that he was to die in the jungle had brought him to a state approaching insanity, and only the shouting of the men pulling the bullock carts had saved him.

By the beginning of June over fifty per cent of personnel were so sick that they were beyond work, and the remainder were suffering from the usual malarial attacks and the everpresent intestinal complaints. For the non-workers we continued to receive only fifty per cent of the normal ration-issue but, of course, everyone received equal amounts at meal-times. We had the good fortune at this time to find some old bullocks at the roadside. They appeared to have been abandoned because they were too old to work. We dispatched them as mercifully as possible and had meat stew for both Jungle and ourselves, but it was tough and insipid meat and I suspect it made a greater contribution to our palates than to our welfare.

The snake population now began to suffer fairly heavily. In earlier times we had avoided them on the grounds that they could only be harmful but we now saw them as a source of nutrition. We lay in wait for them on their nocturnal excursion through the hut and, at a given signal, pounced. Few of them got away. We hung them up until their post-mortem writhing ceased, chopped them into cutlets, and grilled them over a bamboo fire. They were as tasty as chicken and much more palatable than the poor old bullocks.

On 2 July 1945 I noted in my diary that of the 186 men in Tagare only fifteen were going out to work – and even the Japanese recognized that their customary threats and beatings were pointless. Both morbidity and mortality rates were higher than most of us had experienced on the railway, and most of those who died were so wasted by starvation and sickness that we could put them in rice-bags for burial. We made a clearing nearby in the jungle and buried our friends as deeply as the terrain would allow. As we had no padre and no prayer book we simply said the Lord's prayer over their graves and added our own personal farewells. Many of these people had been known to us throughout our service lives, and it was heart-breaking to see them reduced to shrunken cadavers, all the soft tissue gone and, where they had died on their backs, their eye sockets filled with fluid, presumably from their tear-ducts, and their eyes totally submerged.

The greatest tragedy lay in the fact that, having fought so valiantly and for so long, we were within sight of freedom, without knowing it. If we had known that the war in Europe was over and that the Japanese were being battered into submission on land and sea I think that many would have been given the will to continue the fight.

In those final weeks of the war the Japanese displayed a callousness that was totally and frighteningly inhuman, even by their long-established standards. They moved the acutely sick into a 'camp' on the other side of the river, where they were to be given 'special treatment' and we were forbidden to go near it. When we ignored this order and crossed the river on foot in the higher reaches the reason for their proscription was hideously apparent. Both camps were swarming with mosquitoes, rats and leeches, but the huts in the hospital camp were without roofs and the inhabitants were lying naked in the pouring rain with no treatment and minimal food and water.

There was nothing we could do to help them. I hadn't had a medical bag for several months, and the entire provision of a medical nature was a two ounce bottle of Eusol and an old pen-knife. An engine room artificer whom I had know for some years asked me to lance a huge pus-filled boil on the top of his spine as he couldn't stand the pain and headache that this was causing. Under protest, and having explained the hazards, I obliged – and he died the following day. This theme of sudden death continued in both camps. We had an older man, who was reputed to be an ex-regular soldier, who had delighted audiences with his lectures on the old taverns of London. He assured me that he would be home in London in the following February to celebrate his wedding anniversary. I told him that our health was so bad and we carried so many diseases that even if we were freed on the morrow we would never reach England by February. He died overnight – and I was married in England in the following February!

A New Zealander with whom I had formed a good friendship on the Mergui, and I, carried a huge load of goods to a Japanese supply dump, a journey that took the better part of a day and covered many miles. We were both delighted with our achievement. On the following day he dropped dead as he was crossing the camp.

In this same camp I met a man from my home town who was a manager of a clothing shop, from which I had bought a coat just before the war. Most of his right cheek, arm and leg had been sliced off by a Japanese officer with his sword when the poor fellow was standing at attention on parade. He developed severe amoebic dysentery and we carried him to the latrine many times until the Japanese insisted that he 'cross the river'. Within a day or two he was found dead on his bed.

However, the strangest case concerned an Australian, known to everyone, inevitably, as Bluey. He was a man of wide interests, well-read, a ham operator in Australia, and of a happy and confident disposition. One day he turned to several of his closest friends and began to distribute his few remaining treasures. When they questioned the reason he told them that on Thursday at noon he would die. As this was several days away, they told him to keep his posses- sions, promising that if the worst came to the worst they would accept his gifts as he had presented them. On Thursday precisely at noon he lay back on his bed, dead; and they fulfilled their promise.

By 1 August 1945 all my close friends were either dead or had been moved down-country by the Japanese, ostensibly on their way to treatment in hospital. The camp malaria was so bad that, on the recommendation of our Javanese friends, we cut the creepers from the trees and made an infusion similar to quinine in order to try to mitigate the worst symptoms. It made a very unpleasant drink but the experiment didn't last long enough to be proved one way or the other.

At about this time I had one of the worst experiences of the entire period of captivity. I learnt later that the Japanese sergeant involved had planned to go fishing and swimming and had been very upset when an officer had instructed him to take charge of a party. He was also reported to have drunk a considerable amount of alcohol, possibly saki.

I was part of a team involved in road-building when he suddenly made a violent attack on me with a garden spade. The more I tried to evade the blows on the whole of my body the more violent he became and I was soon badly bruised and bleeding profusely. He threw down the spade and immediately picked up a full-size tree-axe, which he proceeded to whirl over his and my heads, while he screamed unintelligible abuse. I stood my ground – in abject fear – because I realised that if I ran he would probably split my skull from behind and say that I was running away. Eventually he threw the axe down, by which time my left arm was hanging uselessly.

We had collected a supply of boulders at the side of the road, and I was now ordered to transfer these to the other side of the road about thirty feet away. As I had only one arm, I had to kneel in the mud, drag each one up my bare thighs and lug it across to the other side. After transporting several dozens I was then ordered to put them all back on the original site! By the time this was done my hands and thighs were scraped raw and bleeding. My friends agreed that I was probably the nearest six-footer when his brainstorm started.

At least we were now beginning to see both reason and reward for our recent efforts. Each day brought a tatterdemalion throng of Japanese and Korean troops in headlong retreat from the Allied forces working south through Burma. Gone were the arrogance and marching songs of former years. They were as happy to retreat from the bombs and guns as we had been three and a half years before. Some idea of the speed of their retreat could be gleaned from their general appearance. Several were without trousers and footwear, they were obviously both hungry and thirsty, and they were without personal kit of any kind.

The callousness with which our camp guards treated their fleeing comrades was almost beyond belief. We POWs had survived the appalling conditions of captivity by interdependence and comradeship of the most generous and compassionate kind. The guards saw their compatriots as traitors and cowards fleeing before the enemy. I never saw a drink of water, a mouthful of food or a cigarette offered, nor heard a word of sympathy. If this was the product of Shintoism, Buddhism and the code of the Samurai, one was forced to wonder what the outcome of our earlier experience would have been if Britain hadn't already been totally committed in Europe, and the Japanese hadn't attacked Pearl Harbour and Singapore without a declaration of war.

On these occasions, pathos and bathos were in sharp contention. It is impossible, in terms of modern warfare, to think of anything more ludicrous than a fully-grown elephant dragging through the mud a small field-gun marked Battle of Adowa 1896 – obviously a present from Mussolini to the Far Eastern member of the Axis. Perhaps it came from the same museum as those similarly-marked rifles from which, in 1942, we had removed the firing pins before allowing them to continue their journey to the Japanese in Burma.

One remembers a Japanese officer – all five feet of him – sitting in exemplary dignity on his horse, the while it fought hock-deep through mud. Bearing in mind its suffering through a deep laceration of its belly, and the attendant torment of flies and sweat, it seemed that the horse's dignity outshone that of its rider by a factor of several thousand. If he had had the humanity to walk he would have lost face!

Although we knew nothing of the progress of the Far Eastern war, or even of events in Europe, we could place only one interpretation on the scenario in our immediate vicinity. Worn-out, over-crowded lorries, exhausted and dispirited troops, and the total absence of any fighting within earshot, meant only one thing and only one possible destination – the Japanese homeland via Prachuab, and the final defence by an army quitting the area of its most-treasured conquests.

After so many false rumours and frustrated hopes it would have been naive of us to see these signs as heralding an early end to the war. Providing the Japanese had the war material necessary for such a campaign we recognised only too clearly that they were capable of fighting even more tenaciously for their Motherland and their Emperor than they had been for their far-flung and short-lived Empire; and our own survival in such an event occupied our thoughts to a considerable degree.

By early August we had fifty-seven men in camp, of whom two were on normal work and four on light work. The remainder had been transferred to our so-called hospital across the river which now had a hundred occupants, all more or less awaiting the Great Reaper, as any form of treatment was out of the question. And each day we crossed the river, encouraged the living, and buried the dead.

How strange some of the entries now seem after forty-odd years of peace. 10 August was my fiancée's birthday, and I followed time-honoured tradition by looking at my now-tatty photo of her, and reading the only four, and by now archaic, letters I had been allowed to receive in three-and-a-half years. Thanks to the generosity of a friend I washed my hands and face very sparingly with soap – in cold water, of course – for the first time in several months. Further to celebrate the occasion I bought two peanut biscuits for breakfast; and in the evening, around a guttering pig-oil lamp, three of us shared peanut biscuits, Eccles cake, and a piece of Chinese wedding-cake – at the expense of two of my generous friends. I never asked the source of such gifts but they must have involved considerable sacrifice for both.

We were now on the very shortest of short commons; for breakfast a quarter pint of pap rice, for lunch a quarter pint of thin marrow-water with a small amount of rice, and half a pint of the same for dinner, with occasional flavourings of pork or beef. Our beriberi and pellagra worsened, our dizziness and breathlessness increased, and the rigors of malaria were more frequent and more prolonged. We would have been superhuman to have withstood the pressures of ill-health and starvation, slave labour, physical violence, the constant torrential rain, lack of sunshine, the presence of rats, bamboo lice and bugs, and, for those who were addicted, the almost total lack of tobacco, without suffering from some form of mental reaction. Acute depression, loss of concentration and memory, and a tendency to lose one's temper over what would otherwise have been seen as minutiae were common; and intractable depression has been a frequent illness among ex-POWs in the post-war years – and still is.

At all times, as has already been said, it seemed that the

war would never end, and the Japanese would repeat to us what had obviously been told by higher authority: that India had collapsed and was now part of their Empire, that Australia and America had been successfully invaded and were suing for peace, and that England had been almost wiped out by German rockets.

In the silly lingua franca that we had created over the years, we would reply: "Squashi mati mati, takusan English squawki bom bom bom Nippon", (Wait a little while, big English planes will bomb Japan), little realising what terrible and condign punishment our prophecy involved. We sought distraction and comfort from many sources: our friends, our Bibles, our prayers, the learning of poetry, the writing of a non-stop letter to those at home; anything that would provide distraction between one sleep and another.

As with alcohol in the earliest days, those with an addiction to tobacco were probably the greatest sufferers. Their craving, while not providing a basis for suicide, certainly lessened their resistance to surrounding pressures, and diminished their will-power.

On returning to camp one evening from the day's labours, I saw an English soldier sitting by a huge campfire, looking the very picture of dejection. When I asked the reason he said that he had no tobacco and that he would cut his throat if none were forthcoming by lights-out; and indicated his open clasp-knife at his side. In a reply sadly lacking in Christian charity I advised him to save himself a few hours of misery by doing it immediately as there was no tobacco in any form in the camp.

When I saw him later his face was wreathed in smiles. When I asked him the source of his anodyne he replied, 'I cut the crown out of my bloody felt hat and smoked that; and I've got more for tomorrow!' And there was his old bush hat, sweat-soaked and filthy after four years of hard use, with its crown missing.

Owing to weakness, hunger and the mud and almost continuous rain, we were all now approaching total immobility. In early August I was asked by one of our MOs if I would help him to carry half-a-bucket of cooked rice from the cooking point 200 yards away, as there was no one else sufficiently mobile to make the journey and carry the rice.

He was a young man who was carrying a burden too great either for his years or his medical qualifications. He was one of the most conscientious people I have ever met in my entire life, and it was obvious that his deep distress was occasioned by the loss of so many people whose treatment would have been relatively easy if the Japanese had had the humanity to make the means available. I readily complied with his request and on the return journey with the rice he told me that in his opinion we should all shortly be dead, as, quite apart from disease, there would be no-one strong enough in camp to cook, carry and serve the food – even though our number had now dwindled to fifty two all-told. I told him, admittedly without a great deal of conviction, that I had no intention of fulfilling his prophecy.

On 18 August 1945 at 1330 hours we were told by our hosts that all walking sick were to leave for Manoa camp immediately after tiffin; but at 1430 hours one of my friends who had supplied the supper on 10 August said, 'Listen chaps, I've just been given some news by the Japanese. It may not be of interest to all of you, of course. The war is over and we're all free!'

Despite the variants of this theme that we had heard over the years, this statement had the undeniable ring of truth, and we accepted it without question. Our yell of delight was heard by those people 200 yards away in the jungle. This was followed by 'The King', and one minute's silence for our dead and two prayers of gratitude for our survival and manumission.

At 1600 hours we had our moment of glory, and put a bit of salt in the Japanese wound. The large Union flag, under which we had buried most of our dead, and which the Japanese had sought in vain, was fastened to the top of a ten foot bamboo pole, and led the way out of the camp, to the enormous chagrin of our enemies; I freed my gold ring from its recent tangle of string and broken needles, and put it back on my finger, to their further annoyance.

Thanks mainly to death but partly to dispersal through sickness to lower camps, there were only fifty-two of the original 500 in Moaner's Creak when freedom came. Thus in four months the Japanese had achieved what even the disastrous Railway of Death had failed to do – a death rate of almost eighty per cent, as it was subsequently stated that only 204 of the original 1000 had survived. I have no means of confirming those figures and they are given in good faith only.

Although we had only sixteen kilometres (ten miles) to cover to the next camp the journey taxed our mental and physical resources to the extreme limit. All of us were sick, and in a civilised environment would have been undergoing hospital treatment. We were plagued by sandfly and leeches, the road was deep in mud, and , as usual, we were in bare feet.

On that day of release I had my nineteenth day of malaria non-stop, untreated by quinine, and with the usual high temperature and shakes. I soon realised that I would find difficulty in reaching the next camp, and began to regret my refusal of the MO's offer of transport. When I fell, which was increasingly frequently, I had the greatest difficulty in regaining my feet. At last I was forced to accept that I could go no further, and as I was the last man of that contingent, there was no-one whom I could ask to carry a message for me.

At about 2200 hours I lay down in the shelter of a fallen tree and prepared to spend the night there. However, in a little while I heard what was obviously a search party, and was able to tell two British POWs and an armed Japanese soldier that they need go no further as I was the last man. Thus it was that I reached yet another camp, at 2300 hours, Moulton Ration Camp, and was welcomed with pork and bean stew. Thanks to a reason which was as yet obscure, our release had been so precipitate that the Allies had not yet caught up with us but the suggestion was subsequently made that the Japanese had refused to reveal our where-abouts because of our enormous death-rate and the starving condition of the survivors. This may also have been the reason for the stew, as until then we had continued to live off manure rice and dried vegetables. It is worth recording that before the reason for the cessation of hostilities was known the Japanese had threatened dire punishments if we revealed to our liberators that the Japanese had eaten all the fresh vegetables, and we all the dried throughout the Mergui stint, obviously against regulations.

I had a most illuminating experience during the march to the Moulton camp. During the afternoon I met a Chinaman whom I now believe to have been a member of the Special Operations Executive, whose presence was unknown to us as captives. He told me that the European war had been over since early May, that Churchill was no longer premier but had been replaced by Attlee, and that Roosevelt was dead and had been replaced by Truman. He was vague about the cause of the sudden end to the war, but repeated the story of a massive explosion and thought that the Japanese had surrendered. Certainly the Japanese psyche had been severely bruised; gone were the bombast and the strident arrogance, and in their place were quiet introspection and depression. Perhaps they realised at last that they weren't the world-conquering heroes that their leaders had cracked them up to be, but rather the representatives of a shoddy little country that had attacked its former friends when victory seemed easy, and had employed every artifice of aggression – torture, rape, murder, starvation, tropical disease, forced labour and violent duress in order to advance its ill-gotten empire. If any evidence is needed to underwrite this statement, take stock of the number and volume of graves in every area of Japanese aggression – and bear in mind that the majority of the occupants were killed, not in the heat of battle, but in the slow and purposeful torture of the labour camps; or as with those nurses who were captured on their way to Sumatra as Singapore fell and were driven into the sea and machine-gunned to death. If this was the spirit of Bushido with its claim of magnanimity towards the enemy and chivalry towards its captives then it bore a striking resemblance to the axis policy on the other side of the world, with its 'final solution' via the gas chamber, execution squads, and the squalor of Belsen, Buchenwald and all the other symbols of man's moral collapse.

It was part of the enormous tragedy of this whole episode that, even though we were now free, deaths continued at the previous rate, and sickness took over the entire camp. Malaria, dysentery and advanced beriberi were so rife that there was no-one to dig latrines, and water was almost unobtainable, either as cookhouse issue or from an adjoining river, which we could have boiled for ourselves. The river was too far away to be accessible to sick men, and only sufficient could be collected each day for the cooking of rice. Yet again we were faced with overflowing latrines, open swill-pits, and vast armies of flies, blue-bottles and mosquitoes.

On 27 August we had recuperated sufficiently to be allowed to move again, and for the first time for four-and-a-half months we left the jungle and came out into the open at the Railway Camp, where we had our midday meal. From there we marched to Kroan camp, which was the mustering centre for all the troops who had been on the Mergui Road. There I had the great pleasure of re-meeting several old friends – Henson, Harrison, Stinson, and others – but a tally of the known dead soon revealed the enormous gaps in our ranks.

These gaps became even more apparent when I was given charge of the newly created Orderly Room, consisting of three clerks and a runner. Our task was to prepare a nominal roll of all survivors, so that flight schedules could be prepared for the trip to Rangoon. This was a most frustrating and unhappy task and lists had constantly to be amended as deaths occurred. It would be difficult to imagine anything worse than for next-of-kin to be told that their loved ones had survived, only to find this subsequently to be erroneous.

We were now given abundant evidence that much of the sickness and many of the deaths of the last few years could have been avoided. In order to save their miserable skins the Japanese now began to issue quinine, emetine, other drugs and dressings that had been stored in Bangkok for more than three years – and the main hospital camp – Na Kompaton – was on the line between Bangkok and ourselves. Equally miraculously, on this tiny camp on the edge of the jungle, we were issued with boots, socks, toothbrush and paste, cigarettes – all by courtesy of our former hosts.

Throughout most of the last four months we had had a particularly odious Korean guard who had done everything possible to inflict suffering and hunger on his captives. This travesty of human existence now became the runner

165

between the Japanese office and my own. As might be expected now that the tables were turned, he was as ingratiating and unctuous as Uriah Heep at his worst, saluting, bowing and standing rigidly to attention whenever he approached us. I took a fiendish delight in issuing one sheet of paper when he asked for twenty, and calling him every name in the book (which he well understood) and provoked him in every way possible to attack me. He was as humble as a lamb, and the very picture of self-abnegation. As I was then less than six stones he could have eliminated me with one hand!

Probably everyone in the camp had some sort of physical problem, and quite a few a mental one as well. The prevalent ones were dysentery, malaria, beriberi, and non-specific diarrhoea, all of which had been our constant companions for three and a half years. The sight and hearing problems had certainly increased during our stay in Siam. In 1985 the assembled ex-POWs in London were informed by the Director of St Dunstan's that he still had 200 ex-POWs in his care – after forty years! The memorable phrase of one of our MOs that the 'light of the countenance had gone out', as the men were overcome by devastating circumstances, was capable of more than one interpretation. Apart from malaria, my main problem was of episodes of total deafness, and these gradually resolved, with improved diet, into the poor level of hearing that plagues me today.

On 1 September we were allowed to write our first letters home – twenty-five words after almost four years – and I was appointed censoring officer. There were no envelopes, of course, and the paper was sealed with liquid rice. As the war was now over and I couldn't think of a single thing that an ex-POW might say that would re-start the war or sour international relations I countersigned them all without reading a single word and sent them on their journey for despatch by air.

On 3 September Liberators overflew Kirikhan aerodrome six kilometres away, and dropped long-awaited supplies of soap, money, cigarettes, drugs, etc., and these were followed shortly by paratroops, many of whom had fought throughout the entire war. These battle-hardened warriors were so appalled by our condition, and conditions, that they went to the periphery of the camp and were physically sick. All of them complained that we stank, (not surprising after three and a half years without hot water and soap), and one said he had been at the opening of Belsen (which meant nothing to us), and he had seen nothing worse there.

We were quite literally astonished one morning to see a whole convoy of vans loaded with chickens, pigs, fruit, and vegetables pass the perimeter of our unfenced camp, and assumed that these were intended for our liberators. Within a short while we were emulating the Bisto Kids, as long-forgotten culinary fragrances began to drift through our quarters, and in due course we were invited to 'come and eat as much as you want'. In my excitement my first chicken-leg slipped out of my fingers and I began to wipe the sand and grit off it. It was taken from me, and a clean one substituted, with the assurance that I could have as many as I could eat.

The reason for this banquet only became apparent later. A paratroop major who had dropped into the area at breakfast-time had asked one of our fellows what he was eating.

'Kachang-iju, sir'

'Kachang-iju! What the hell's that?'

'Peas, sir, one of our favourite dishes, boiled with sugar – we don't often get it.'

The major threw the mess-tin into the jungle, drew his revolver, and told the Japanese guard commander that unless plentiful food was forthcoming within the hour he would shoot the entire guard, one by one.

It was!

One of the major drawbacks of our tardy return to the coast was that I never had the opportunity to say goodbye to our faithful companion, Jungle. I learned from others that he was in a poor state physically, but that his spirit was undimmed. I hope with all my heart that he returned to his family and was there nursed back to health with all the love that he so richly deserved. For many years I have felt that in a contest between humans and animals for a display of Christian virtues, animals are easy victors, and Jungle exemplified that conviction.

It is one of the ironies of existence that we have now achieved almost half a century of peace because we possess the means of mass destruction of such horrendous proportions that no one has dared to employ it since 1945.

The political ideology that would eliminate the hydrogen bomb unilaterally is so misguided that it is difficult to believe that intelligent people would discard so effective an insurance policy, and by so doing run the risk of the very conditions that are so well-known to the war generation: loss of liberty, genocide, starvation, rape, torture and epidemic disease.

How evident it is that most of our modern politicians have no memory of war, have never heard a shot fired in anger, nor seen the result of mass urban bombing, except in pictures. One genius even advanced the theory that conventional weapons were permissible, as though suffering were any less for being inflicted by bombs, bullets, mustard gas and burns. He had obviously never seen the limbless, the blind and the burnt in their dying agony, nor listened to their screams as they approached the Grim Reaper.

Stalin and Hitler were not the last of their breed; indeed they have been replicated many times in the intervening years and they are with us today. Vietnam, Khmer Rouge, the rape of Czechoslovakia and Hungary, Beirut, the Falklands, Iran/Iraq, Libya and Chad are all evidence of a wider blood-lust and we ignore it at our peril. The bully will always attack the weakest of the species and those who are unable or unwilling to defend themselves. The Romans proved it 2,000 years ago and any who ignore it risk the liberty and well-being of those they manipulate – either for political advantage or personal gain: 'If you wish for peace prepare for war.'   It is as true today as it was then; by the same token it is a very short step from those who would ban the bomb in its entirety to those who profess to mourn each year for those who suffered so grievously in Hiroshima and Nagasaki.

I doubt if there is a person in the world who would not ban the bomb if there were a guarantee that it could be done on a global basis and perpetuated. So long as there are human nature, politics and religion there will be wars, however dreadful the means of destruction.

For the vast majority of FEPOWs those who mourn the Japanese suffering are seen as exhibitionists and hypocrites whose false nobility of character does them little credit.

They should bear in mind four things:

(1) The Japanese started the war when they thought victory would be easy.
(2) The military and civilian graveyards of South East Asia are full of the victims of Japanese genocide; and homes all over the world house the victims of Japanese torture and neglect.
(3) If the bombs had not been dropped on Hiroshima and Nagasaki thousands of military and civilian personnel would have been bayonetted to death.
(4) If the war had been carried to the invasion of the Japanese mainland by sea and airborne attack countless thousands would have died on both sides.

7

WE'LL MEET AGAIN . . .

On 2 September evacuation by air from Kirikhan aerodrome commenced. I agreed to stay behind to supervise the
loading of the planes from our nominal rolls, an easy task as
we now had our lists up-to-date. Flights continued on a
daily basis and on the 7 September I left Kirikhan on an
ancient workhorse – the Dakota, so dearly loved by all
whom those wonderful craft served throughout the greater
part of the war. She had no seats, and her polished
aluminium floor bore witness to her work over the dropping
zones of Burma.

With each phase of freedom that we passed through our
spirits became more buoyant, our convalescence more
evident, and our excitement more intense. On 6 September
we had another anti-cholera injection, (British, now), and
went through that rather humiliating experience of passing
through a long hut, the while removing our buggy, lousy
and dirty possessions, passing naked to the next section,
and emerging in green drill kit complete with soap, towel,
and cigarettes. Now we could face the civilized world again.

We left at 1350 hours, flew at 130 mph over the remains
of our railway, encountered rain and low cloud in the
middle of our journey, and emerged into bright and clear
weather to land at Mingaladon aerodrome, north east of
Rangoon, at 1730 hours. For the last twenty-five minutes of
the flight I sat next to the pilot, who said that his 'old crate'
was tied together with string, had been flying over the
Hump into China throughout the war, and was now almost
ready for the scrap-heap. At least she served our purpose
well, gave me magnificent views of the limpid waters of the
Gulf of Martaban and the golden dome of the Shwe Dagon

pagoda, and landed us safely. (We were horrified to learn that one of these planes laden with over thirty POWs, on their way to freedom, had crashed, and all aboard had been killed).

We had tea with milk and sugar, bread, butter, and cheese, and spoke to a white woman. Was it really three-and-a-half years since we had last had these experiences?

My first disappointment came when I was admitted to a tented ward at the British Military Hospital, Rangoon. After a detailed examination I was told that I must stay on my bed throughout each day, and that this was not to be broken either for food or toilet. I told the lady MO that a few weeks previously I had been carrying trees single-handed, to which she replied that that was all the more reason for resting; and added that I probably wouldn't be allowed home for several weeks because of severe beriberi and malaria. As I was the only one in the ward under these strictures, I felt rather aggrieved.

On the following day, after ward rounds, I was informed that there was a notice-board announcement that all valuables handed to the Japanese in the previous year could be collected from an office on the Prome road, about five miles away. I took French leave, and in scorching heat, with my new clothes and footwear chafing, I collected all my valuables. I was able to hand to the officer in charge many dozens of parcels of people who had died in the intervening months, many of them my friends of several years' duration.

We were now told officially that examination of Japanese papers had revealed that all senior commanders in the field had been instructed to destroy all POWs and civilian internees commencing on 23 August 1945. After three-and-a-half years of captivity we had been released with five days to spare – a little bit too close for comfort. As it was unlikely that so late in the war the Japanese would have expended valuable amunition on their victims, one assumes that their preferred method would have been by sword and bayonet – much more rewarding to the executioner in terms of the pain, anguish and blood of his victims.

My hopes of an early move rose dramatically on 10 September when it was announced to the entire ward that we were to move en bloc to the docks and a troopship. We packed as quickly as possible – until Nemesis in the shape of our lady doctor appeared and ordered me back on to my charpoy. When the others had gone, I asked her why, and she told me that my heart was so bad that I would never reach England. Now I was the only occupant of the ward, and remained so.

But it is a poor soldier who can't outwit military discipline. On 15 September my name was called from yet another roll – so I packed and left the ward as quickly as possible. I entered the first fully-laden lorry, hid inside, and asked the fellows to deny any knowledge of me when Nemesis inevitably appeared. This they did, and shortly thereafter I was on my way to Rangoon docks.

Now we could see some of the enormous damage that, repeated throughout South East Asia on a vast scale, had brought Japan to its knees. The atomic bombs on Hiroshima and Nagasaki had obviously forced the decision to surrender so ignominiously but the scale of destruction was so vast around Rangoon that one is forced to the conclusion that, even without the atomic bombs, if all the Allied forces in the Far East had been concentrated on the Japanese Islands the result would have been an early and foregone conclusion. Courage is a poor defence against devastation on so vast a scale. The marshalling yards of the Burmese Railways were simply graveyards for thousands of engines, coaches and trucks, signalling equipment lay in ruins, and the streets and harbour were littered with the debris of war.

Our troop ship was the *Worcestershire*, 17,000 tons, reputed to have been an armed merchantman throughout the war and now converted partly to a hospital ship. Draft 73 joined her on 17 September, and the 1500 men on board, consisting of ex-FEPOWs and 14th Army, now really began to believe that the war was over and we were homeward bound.

We left harbour on the following day at 1145 hours to the accompaniment of heavy rain and rough seas, and as in 1941, were allocated hammocks and table-tops – on D deck. I suppose it was a wise precaution to have boat stations and lifeboat drill because of the risk of mines, but it irked us to continue with picquets, deck-sweeping and mess-orderly duties.

Thirty hours of sea-sickness between 19 and 20 September was probably caused as much by failure to absorb the European food, after years on the plain fare of boiled rice, as it was by the rough sea. The food was varied, plentiful and well-cooked, and we disgusted ourselved with our enormous appetites. We were looking for the next meal almost before the last one was finished, and beverages were available between all meals.

On 22 September I met on deck my MO from Mergui Road, he with whom I had carried the rice in those last days of captivity. Although I assured him that I was greatly improved, he expressed concern at my continuing beriberi, deafness and malaria, and took a blood sample. The count revealed 1,700,000 red blood cells – about one third of normal – and he pooh-poohed this as mistaken. When exactly the same figure was reached on the following day he ordered my immediate admission to the ward.

On that same day we entered Colombo harbour in totally unforgettable circumstances. Short of the harbour a Royal Naval pinnace came out to meet us bearing a huge message of welcome held by the crew; and as we made harbour the assembled navies of the Allied Powers – battleships, cruisers, carriers, frigates and corvettes sounded the V for victory on their sirens, and flashed it by Aldis lamp. The shore searchlights not only formed a V skyward, but flashed those same lights in the well-known three dots and a dash of the Morse code, an enormous orchestration of welcome benediction against the background of a full tropical moon. We acknowledged it by every means possible from our ship.

So on 23 September I was warded, to join those others who were now discovering all sorts of weird conditions previously unsuspected. Apart from severe anaemia, I was diagnosed as suffering from hookworm (thanks to wading barefoot in Siamese rivers), E. coli cysts in my intestines, malaria, dysentery, and atrophic glossitis. A newly-imported MO from the UK greeted me with the phrase. 'You're the corpse who won't admit that you're dead' – and proceeded to bombard me with much of the pharma-copoeia. At least it worked, and with the drugs supplemented by soup, one pound of liver, several rashers of bacon, two vegetables, sweet and beverage, I began to make rapid strides to normal health.

That meal, of course, was only lunch. We had a cooked breakfast of sausage, bacon and eggs, a cooked dinner at night and a beverage at lights out. We all suffered from the same insatiable appetite which, in my case, was nearly my undoing. We were issued with a tin of K rations – an American product outside of our previous experience and which contained no instructions. In a moment of hunger late one evening I ate from the tin what I took to be oatmeal cake. Within a short while I was suffering the most severe thirst and indigestion of my life. The more I drank the worse the pain became,and I was aware of a quite severe abdominal swelling. A sympathetic member of the 14th Army, who had spent some time in battle conditions in the jungle, explained that I had eaten a whole cake of porridge, intended to make nine meals of that delectable breakfast – at one sitting and without the benefit of milk, sugar or salt. My distended gastric system was painful for several days thereafter.

We passed the time on our journey up the Indian Ocean and into the Red Sea by completing several more pages of atrocity forms. It was a difficult and tasteless task and almost impossible for those of us who had been fully mobile throughout the building of the railway. In twenty-six camps we had come across several hundreds of Japanese and the pace of the work throughout long hours in squalid conditions, and the resultant exhaustion, had left us with little enthusiasm for determining the identities of our tormentors. Most of them were known throughout the camps by less-than-flattering pseudonyms – the Undertaker, the Silver Bullet, Gonorrhoea, etc. – and only those whose excesses were above average were known by their given names. These were usually officers or senior NCOs, and all of them had moved to the war front in Burma or elsewhere so our evidence did little to bring them to justice.

On 4 October we anchored at Adabiya, and were issued with up-to-date letters, kit to European standards, and various comforts. How overwhelming and miraculous it was to learn that my family had survived the war intact, and that

I now had a niece of fourteen months! My good fortune was in sharp contrast to the many people who now learned of the loss by enemy action of whole families at home, of brothers and sisters killed while on active service, and of wives and sweethearts who had decamped with other men during those uncommunicating years.

Who can blame them? The news was unrelentingly bad from the POW areas throughout the Far East and even the Foreign Secretary announced in the House of Commons that our chances of survival were remote because of the appalling bestiality of the Japanese. But by contrast it is a tribute to those who kept their faith steadfast throughout and were awaiting us after six years and one month of separation.

Our approach to the British Isles was delayed by a symptom that was to become distressingly familiar in the succeeding years and which, ironically, has given the Japanese industrial and commercial dominance of this country – strikes, in this case by the dock workers.

When we dropped anchor in the Mersey on 15 October we were further delayed by dense fog which prevented our docking until the following day. We were greeted by military bands and bunting and huge crowds on the quayside, and further crowds with flags on the streets on the way to Maghull school where we were billeted for the night.

I have already said that there are some experiences that are so indelibly written on the mind that they last as long as life itself. I asked the taxi-driver who took me home from the station to switch off his engine and coast to the gate. I went into the garden, climbed on the window-sill and looked through a gap in the curtains. Suddenly all became justified and worthwhile – all the separation and disease and violence – for there they all were: my family, – the old and the newly acquired, my fiancée with whom my future was to be so richly blessed – and the knowledge that the only absentee, my brother, was safe and sound with the Royal Navy in Singapore.

Singapore – of all places!